A SPACE AGE COOKBOOK FOR KIDS

A SPACE AGE COOKBOOK FOR KIDS

by Shirley Parenteau
and
Barbara Douglass

illustrated by
Laura Hartman

Prentice-Hall, Inc., Englewood Cliffs, New Jersey

Printed in the United States of America

Prentice-Hall International, Inc., London
Prentice-Hall of Australia, Pty. Ltd., North Sydney
Prentice-Hall of Canada, Ltd., Toronto
Prentice-Hall of India Private Ltd., New Delhi
Prentice-Hall of Japan, Inc., Tokyo
Prentice-Hall of Southeast Asia Pte. Ltd., Singapore
Whitehall Books Limited, Wellington, New Zealand

10 9 8 7 6 5 4 3 2 1

Library of Congress Cataloging in Publication Data

Douglass, Barbara, 1930–
  A space age cookbook for kids.

  SUMMARY: *Contains recipes and party ideas with space
themes and miscellany of facts, riddles, and stories
about other space.*
  *1. Cookery—Juvenile literature. 2. Astronautics—
Miscellanea—Juvenile literature. [1. Cookery.
2. Astronautics—Miscellanea] I. Parenteau, Shirley,
joint author. II. Maestro, Laura. III. Title.*
TX652.5.D68   641.5   78-20891
ISBN 0-13-823799-9

For Cherie, Scott, David, Teena, and Jessica.   SP

For Phillip and the others.   BD

Note: Astrofacts change frequently because scientists are constantly making new discoveries about our solar system and the universe. When space probes from the United States landed on Venus in late 1978, the discovery of argon gasses in Venus' atmosphere forced scientists to change their theories on how the solar system formed. Even while this book is being printed new information is being learned about many of the facts in it. This is just one of the things that makes studying the universe so exciting.

CONTENTS

The sun is a star. It looks different because it is much closer to the earth than other stars. (Only 93 million miles away)

Mercury, the smallest planet, is even closer to the sun than Earth is. It must be very hot on the side of Mercury that is facing the sun. Like all planets, Mercury rotates (spins) as it revolves around (orbits) the sun.

Our twin planet (almost the same size as Earth) orbits the sun in 225 days, so a year on Venus is shorter than a year on Earth.

Earth is a middle-size planet that rotates once every 24 hours. (So on Earth, one day and night together is 24 hours.) Earth orbits the sun once every 365 days. (So on Earth, one year is 365 days.) Earth has one satellite, known as the moon.

Mars, the red planet has two satellites. A year on Mars is almost twice as long as a year on Earth, since Mars is farther from the sun and takes longer (687 days) to orbit that big star.

STARSHIP STARTERS
Terms and Tips

Exploring space is a great adventure—so is exploring the kitchen. Put the two together and you have the daring astrocook, the most important member of the space crew. Astrocooks prepare wholesome meals that are as important to the astronauts as fuel is to the rockets.

With the help of this book, you can make a Sizzling Star, a Supernova, a Starship and many more tasty foods. Mixed with the recipes, you'll find space stories, jokes, tongue twisters, and riddles like these:

Astroriddle: What do you call a scientist with a bald head? *Astrodome.*

Astroriddle: What do you call someone who reads all the recipes through, washes hands, follows directions, and cleans the kitchen afterward? *Astrocook.*

Before we begin we should make a countdown as astronauts do to make sure all systems are A-OK.

1

Countdown to Cooking Adventure

10: Learn How Equipment Works
Before setting off on a journey into space, astronauts check with their commanders to learn all about the machinery and equipment that will be used on the trip.

Before setting off into the kitchen, astrocooks check with the ship captain or other adult to learn how the kitchen equipment works (they don't want to turn on the airlock instead of the oven by mistake).

Astroriddle: What is the first thing astrocooks put in the kitchen? *Their feet—unless they're in zero gravity, then it may be their hands.*

9: Get Permission
Astronauts never launch without permission from the control tower.

Astrocooks ask the ship captain for permission to use the kitchen and the necessary ingredients.

8: Practice
Astronauts start with short trips, then make longer journeys before being chosen by the commander for a complicated mission.

Astrocooks start with one-star recipes, then move on to those marked with two stars. When they feel ready for three-star recipes, they check first with an adult.

7: Choose a Recipe and Read It
Astronauts decide on a destination, then study charts that show the way.

Astrocooks decide what to make, then read the recipe to find out what utensils and foods will be needed.

They make sure they understand all the directions and ask an adult if they are not sure of the meaning. Then they know how to cook the food they like.

Astroriddle: Captain, navigator, engineer, cook—which of the space crew is the meanest? *The cook—he beats some dishes and whips others.*

6: Assemble Your Equipment

Astronauts make a last minute check to be sure all equipment is on hand.

Astrocooks read the recipe again and take out all needed utensils and ingredients. That way you have them when you need them and where you need them. Your hands are an important part of the equipment. Always wash them before handling food.

Astroriddle: What happened to the astrocook who tried to handle too many things at once? *She swallowed the mixing spoon, then wasn't able to stir.*

5: Follow Directions Closely

Astronauts don't want to end up on Jupiter when they have set a course for Mars.

Astrocooks don't want to end up with Sloppy Joe Volcanos when they've planned on making Space Lab Loaf.

4: Keep Safety in Mind

Astronauts follow safety rules when handling their equipment.

Astrocooks do, too. They take care when using knives. They know the ship's doctor is busy tending to people with space sickness and astro-burn, so they don't want to bother the doctor with knife cuts on their hands. When using knives astrocooks always work on cutting boards on a flat surface. They aim the sharp edge away from the hand holding the food and away from their bodies.

When handling hot pans, astrocooks use dry potholders (mitts are even better) to protect themselves from burns. And because steam burns, they open pans by lifting lids away from themselves. They're careful to turn pan handles away from other burners and from the edge of the stove—they don't want to bump the handles by accident and spill the captain's favorite space dish on the floor, or on themselves.

Astroriddle: The astro-library is filled with booktapes. Which do you think has the most stirring chapters? *The cookbook.*

When stirring a pan on the stove astrocooks remember to remove the spoon after stirring the hot mixture. That way the handle won't get too hot to touch.

When they're finished cooking, the astrocooks always take care to turn off their stoves. And if they have to leave the kitchen even for a minute, they turn off all fires on the stove.

3: Clean As You Go

Astronauts keep their starships clean and uncluttered. They put each tool in its proper place when they have finished with it. It's the only way to have a safe, comfortable journey.

Astrocooks wipe up spills right away. They rinse plates, pans, forks, and spoons as soon as they finish with them. (That makes them so much easier to wash.) And the astrocook always cleans the kitchen after using it—unless a household robot is standing by waiting to wash the dishes, countertops, stove, and to sweep the floor.

2: Learn the Language

Astronauts use such terms as fuel emission, cosmic shield, and re-entry.

Astrocooks use such terms as bake, broil, and simmer. These and other common cooking terms are explained later in this chapter under Astrocook Terms.

1: All Systems Go!

You're now set for an adventure through the wide universe of fine foods. Blast off!

Astrofact: Mercury, Venus, Earth, and Mars are called the Terrestrial Planets because they are made of rocky materials. Jupiter, Saturn, Uranus, and Neptune are called the Jovian Planets. They're mostly made of gasses, especially hydrogen and helium, and seem to have the same chemical makeup as the sun. Uranus and Neptune have less hydrogen however and more icy material. Pluto, the outermost planet, is a mystery. It seems to be rocky, or terrestrial (though icy), where we would expect a Jovian-type planet to be located.

Astronauts measure in metrics, but most astrocooks still use cookbooks with old-fashioned Earth measurements. The following shows how to change one to the other.

5

Earth Measure		Metric Measure
1 tbsp (tablespoon)	is the same as	15 ml (milliliters)
1 tsp (teaspoon)	is the same as	5 ml (milliliters)
1 C (cup)	is the same as	240 ml (milliliters)
½ cup	is the same as	120 ml (milliliters)
⅓ cup	is the same as	80 ml (milliliters)
¼ cup	is the same as	60 ml (milliliters)

Sometimes, astrocooks want to make more or less of a favorite recipe. This chart will help.

Equivalents

3 tsp	equal	1 tbsp
4 tbsp	equal	¼ cup
2 cups	equal	1 pint
4 cups	equal	1 quart
4 quarts	equal	1 gallon

Astrotwister: Say this three times fast. Sharon showed Shawn seven shining shrieking starships.

Astrocook Terms

Bake: Cook food in the oven.

Boil: Cook liquid in pan on top of the stove until large bubbles rise over and over again in the liquid.

Broil: Cook food under the broiler of the oven.

Blend: Combine two ingredients, usually by stirring with a spoon.

Simmer: Cook liquid in pan on top of the stove over low heat until tiny bubbles form around the edges of the pan. (Low heat keeps it from boiling.)

Utensils: Pans, skillet, bowls, eggbeaters, mixing spoons—all the tools used for cooking.

Ingredients: Flour, milk, eggs, onions, salt—all the foods and seasonings used for cooking.

Astronutrition Tips

Astronauts and Astrocooks want healthy bodies. So it's good to know that while space scientists are busy learning more about our universe, Earth scientists are busy learning more about what foods are best for building healthy bodies.

For example we know now that white sugar has absolutely no food value.

Astrofact: Using white sugar as fuel for our bodies is as foolish as trying to use cold water as fuel for a rocket.

So astrocooks use honey whenever possible for sweetening. The next best sweeteners are raw sugar, brown sugar, or molasses, but use all sweets sparingly. Most Earth foods are great without them.

Astroreminder: If you can't brush your teeth right away after eating sweets (including raisins and other dried fruits), rinse your mouth well with water. You'll have fewer cavities.

When astrocooks are responsible for shopping, they read labels and avoid foods with a high sugar content and those with chemical additives. They use one of the following in recipes calling for flour:

unbleached flour
or half unbleached flour and half 100% whole wheat flour
or two-thirds unbleached flour and one-third soy flour
or replace two tablespoons flour with two tablespoons wheat germ.

Astrotwister: Say this three times fast: Soy flour stars.

For recipes using bread it's best to choose bread made with 100% whole wheat flour. (Read the ingredients. Some breads labeled "wheat bread" are made with white flour, colored to look like whole wheat.)

When buying peanut butter, read the ingredients. The most nutritious kind—usually labeled "Old-Fashioned"—is made with only peanuts and salt. It is *not* hydrogenated and *no* sugar or corn syrup is added. This wholesome peanut butter must be refrigerated to retain its freshness. Served with milk or milk products, it provides complete protein.

Whenever possible use natural cheese rather than processed types.

Check the label when buying cooking oils too. The most nutritious are 100% vegetable oils. They are *not* hydrogenated, have *no* chemical additives, and must be stored in the refrigerator.

Always cook vegetables, either frozen or fresh, in a small amount of water. (Throwing cooking water away is throwing food value away.) Cook vegetables until just barely tender in a pan with a tight-fitting lid.

Cook canned vegetables by first heating the liquid from the can, then adding the vegetables and heating slowly just a minute or two until they're heated all the way through. Never boil them.

Save cooking water from vegetables to use in homemade soups or add it to canned soups.

Always try to eat at least one raw fruit or vegetable every day. If it is one that must be peeled or cut, do that just before you eat it.

Astroriddle: Which is the bluest side of a grape grown on the third planet from our sun? *The outside.*

STARSHIP STARTERS PUZZLE

Across:
1. What's the first thing you should do with a new recipe?
4. Directions on how to cook a food.
7. Old-fashioned peanut butter gives you complete protein when served with what beverage?
8. Before you begin to cook, get out all your _____.
9. When lunch is usually served.

Down:
1. Eat at least one _____ fruit or vegetable every day.
2. Before cooking, read all _____.
3. When you use this book, you're a good astro_____.
5. The way good astrocooks leave the kitchen.
6. Good food is as important to the crew as _____ is to the rocket engine.
7. What kind of measurement is a milliliter?

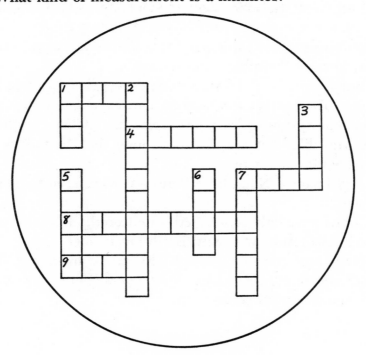

SUN SOLAR SPECIALS
Breakfast Ideas

Earth Must Win!

The Great Galactic Cooking Contest was to be the most exciting event since space travel. Alex was proud to have been chosen best astrocook from Earth. He could hardly wait to meet the other contestants.

But as time for the final contest drew near, Alex began to worry. The contest was held on Earth's moon, with judges from many planets. The newest solar-run kitchen equipment was available. But Alex heard a rumor that the judges had already picked a winner.

A girl named Nomi from Pluto was whispered to be sure to win.

"Maybe it's only gossip," Alex muttered. "But what if it's true? Earth must win. And Earth means me."

Nomi was pleasant enough. Everyone liked her. That made Alex more suspicious. Nomi could afford to be nice if she knew she was going to win.

The final contest event was Creative Breakfasts.

"I wonder what Nomi will make," Alex said to himself. "Wouldn't the judges be surprised if I made the same thing? They couldn't choose Nomi over me if our breakfasts were the same. We'd both have to make new recipes."

When he checked the contestant's listing, Alex saw he was scheduled to cook his breakfast idea just ahead of Nomi. "What if I cook the same thing, but I cook it first?" he wondered.

He made up his mind. Even if it was only gossip that Nomi had already been chosen the winner, it made no difference. He'd heard Nomi's breakfast was special. But Earth must win.

Alex made his plans.

During sleeping time, Alex slipped over to Nomi's quarters. He heard her even breathing and knew she was asleep. Then he turned on a micro-light and copied her breakfast recipe from a card in her bag.

At contest time the sky was bright with the clear-aired sharpness so popular on Earth's moon. But Alex didn't glance through the bubble window to admire the shadowed landscape. He was busy creating Nomi's recipe which he renamed "Sizzling Stars, an old family recipe of mine."

He toasted bread, scrambled eggs, cheesed cutout stars, put everything together, and shoved the tray into the solar broiler. Then he set the timer by Nomi's card.

The judges came by just as the timer rang. Alex prepared to take out his creation with a flourish. But when he opened the broiler all he could do was stare.

The stars were not sizzling. They were flaming—over toast and cheese and eggs crisped to charcoal. The stench of burning cheese steamed from the blackened stars.

After a stunned moment Alex realized Nomi was looking over his shoulder. He turned in time to see her smile at the judges.

11

"If you'll look into my broiler, you'll see *my* old family recipe," she said. "With solar cooking time shortened to suit the nearness of Earth's moon to the sun. Pluto is so much farther from solar heat."

Astrofact: The sun is a star. It looks different because it is much closer to the earth than other stars. (Only 93 million miles away.) The sun is the center of our solar system, and breakfast is the center of a good nutrition program.

☆☆ SIZZLING STARS

Here is Nomi's prize-winning recipe—it's a sunny way to start the day.

cheese	*cheese grater*
slice of bread	*table knife*
butter or margarine	*star-shaped cookie cutter*
1 tbsp vegetable oil	*small bowl*
1 egg	*pancake turner*

Grate enough cheese to make a small mound in a tablespoon. Turn oven to 450 degrees. Toast a slice of bread and spread lightly with butter or margarine. Cut out the center with a star-shaped cookie cutter. Spread the star of toast with grated cheese. Heat in the broiler for a minute or two, just until the cheese is sizzling. Turn off oven.

While the cheesy star cools in the broiler, fry the egg: pour tablespoon of oil into skillet and place on the stove over low heat. Break the egg into a bowl. Holding the bowl above the skillet, gently slide the egg into the oil. Cook about 1½ to 2 minutes. (Low heat keeps eggs tender.)

To serve, place cutout slice of toast on a plate. Lift egg from skillet with a pancake turner and place it into the cutout center of the toast. With the pancake turner lift the star from the broiler and place on top of the egg.

To make scrambled eggs in your Sizzling Stars add to above list milk, measuring spoons, and a fork.

Make toast and cheesy star as directed above. Then pour tablespoon of oil into skillet and place on stove over low heat. Break an egg into a small bowl, add tablespoon of milk, and whip milk and egg together with fork. Holding bowl above the skillet, gently slide egg mixture into oil. Stir while cooking until the egg is as firm as you like it. Serve as above. *Serves 1.*

Astroextra: Sizzling Stars are also good for breakfast, lunch, or supper filled with the mixture for Venusian Odyssey (Chapter 4) or Sloppy Joe Volcanoes (Chapter 4).

Astrojoke: The lost astronaut was happy to be rescued and served a plate of Sizzling Stars. How many Stars could he eat when his stomach was completely empty? *One—after that his stomach was not completely empty.*

Astroriddle: Kelly had a boiled egg for breakfast when she visited Uranus. She ate the egg without breaking the shell. How could she do that? *She asked the astrocook to break it for her.*

☆☆ MOON PLATE

Light brown craters puff up in your Moon Plates as they bake. Serve them quickly on hot pads to protect the table.

3 eggs
½ cup flour
½ cup milk
2 tbsp melted butter or
  margarine
½ tsp salt
warm honey, maple syrup,
  fresh fruit or
  other topping

measuring cup and spoons
fork or wire whip
mixing bowl
small pan for melting
  butter
two 9-inch pie pans
waxed paper
potholders or mitts

Using folded waxed paper, rub butter or margarine over insides of pie plates and set aside. Heat oven to 400 degrees. Melt 2 tablespoons butter or margarine in small pan.

Beat eggs in bowl until light and fluffy. Beat in the flour, a little at a time, until all is used. Then beat in the milk, a little at a time. Stir in the melted butter and the salt.

Divide the batter into the two prepared pie plates. Put the plates into the hot oven (keep your face away from the oven door when you first open it—hot air will rush out). Bake for 10 minutes, then turn the oven down to 350 degrees. Bake for 5 minutes more or until the Moon Plates are puffy, with light browned craters. Use potholders or mitts to carry them to your waiting crew. Serve with favorite toppings. *Serves 2.*

Astroriddle: After splashdown in the Pacific Ocean, why is a space capsule like the letter *T*? *It's in the middle of water.*

☆☆☆ SKYWHEEL OMELET

Pork links and omelet ingredients make this Skywheel in a skillet a favorite with the crew.

½ lb pork links
2 eggs
⅛ cup milk
¼ tsp salt
dash Tabasco sauce
4 slices bread
butter or margarine

small (9-inch) skillet
spatula
measuring cup and spoons
mixing bowl
fork or wire whip
knife

Brown pork links in skillet over medium heat. Beginning astrocooks should ask an adult to pour off the hot fat that cooks out of the links. More experienced cooks can carefully spoon the fat into a container. Arrange the links in a spoke formation like a skywheel. (Move them into place with the spatula.) Beat together the eggs, milk, and seasonings.

Slowly pour the egg mixture over the pork links. Cover the pan. Simmer over medium heat for about 5 minutes, or until the omelet is set.

While the omelet is cooking, toast the bread, butter it, and place it on serving dishes. Cut the omelet into four wedges and serve on hot buttered toast. *Serves 4.*

Astrotwister: The sun shines sometimes. Say this five times fast.

☆☆☆ WEIGHTLESS PANCAKES

These pancakes are so light, they almost float off the griddle.

1 egg	*measuring cups and spoons*
1 cup milk	*mixing bowl*
½ tbsp vegetable oil	*eggbeater*
1 cup flour	*griddle*
¼ tsp salt	*large mixing spoon*
1½ tsp baking powder	*or ladle*
butter, margarine, or	*large serving spoon*
sour cream	*pancake turner*
honey or maple syrup	

Place griddle on stove over low heat. Break egg into mixing bowl. Beat with eggbeater until light and fluffy. Add milk and oil and half the flour. Turn heat under griddle up to medium.

Sprinkle salt and baking powder over mixture in bowl. Add the rest of the flour and beat about eight turns with the eggbeater. Wet your fingers and shake a few drops of water onto the griddle. If the water hops about, the griddle is hot enough. Then, with large mixing spoon or ladle, pour three separate spoonfuls of batter on the griddle. As the batter cooks, bubbles will rise. When the pancakes are bubbly all over and the first few bubbles pop, turn pancake over and cook until the bottom is lightly browned.

Makes 12 pancakes to serve with butter, margarine, or sour cream topped with honey or syrup.

Astroextra: Pancakes don't have to be round. When you pour the batter on the griddle you can dribble it to make the shape of a rocket, a flying saucer, a sky lab—anything your imagination may suggest.

16

☆ GALACTIC GOOP

Three easy ways to make a delicious breakfast that's good for you, too.

bread or English muffin   *table knife*
banana   *toaster or griddle*
raisins
butter or margarine

For a grilled Galactic Goop sandwich, use two slices of bread, preferably whole wheat. Spread one slice with butter or margarine. Spread the other slice with peanut butter. (Old-fashioned style is best.) Top the peanut-buttered bread with banana slices and sprinkle on a few raisins. (If you make only one sandwich, you won't need the whole banana. You can eat what's left while you grill the sandwich.)

Heat a griddle or skillet over medium heat. Put both slices of bread together. Spread the outside of the bread with butter or margarine. Grill a few minutes on each side until the bread is crispy brown.

or: Toast one or two slices of bread. Spread with butter or margarine and peanut butter. Top with banana slices and raisins.

or: Toast an English muffin. Spread with the same Galactic Goop.

To make the most of this meal, have a frosty glass of milk with your Galactic Goop. (Peanut butter and milk together provide complete protein.)

Astroextra: Soups, salads and sandwiches are all good breakfast foods. On a sunny summer morning, you might like a dish of cottage cheese with your favorite fruit. Try half a cantaloupe with cottage cheese in the center—it looks like the planet Saturn with a wide ring. You may name this recipe yourself.

Astrofact: The sun and other stars are made of gasses, mostly hydrogen. Most stars rotate or spin as the planets do, but they don't orbit other solar bodies.

☆☆ ZOOM SOUP

On a cold, wintry morning this soup will start you off with a ZOOM! It's especially good with a grilled cheese sandwich.

1 can tomato soup	*small saucepan*
milk	*can opener*
small piece of cheese	*knife*
(about ⅓ inch thick)	*mixing spoon*

In saucepan, mix the contents of one can tomato soup with one can of water, or one can of milk, or one-half can of milk and one-half can of water. Stir. Turn heat on medium. Stir now and then while heating soup, just until tiny bubbles begin to form at the edge of the pan. If soup starts to boil, turn down the heat.

Cut cheese into small chunks. When soup is hot, turn off heat, pour soup carefully into bowls, and sprinkle a few chunks of cheese on top of each bowl. You and your guests can stir the soup until the cheese zooms out with long comet tails. *Serves 4.*

Astroextra: This is also a good recipe for lunch, with a crisp green salad and an icy glass of milk.

Astrofact: The sun makes one complete spin in about 26 Earth days. It only takes 24 hours for Earth to spin all the way around.

☆ BANANA ROCKETS

Banana Rockets lift off your day with a bright honey-sweet start.

2 firm bananas
1 tbsp melted butter or
    margarine
honey

table knife
cutting board
measuring spoon
teaspoon and fork
waxed paper
small baking dish
pastry brush
potholders or mitts

Set oven at 350 degrees. Using folded waxed paper, rub butter or margarine over inside of a small baking dish. Peel bananas and cut them in half lengthwise. Place bananas in baking dish and brush with honey. Place in heated oven and bake for 15 to 20 minutes. They're ready when you can poke a fork into them easily. Use potholders or mitts to remove baking dish. Set it down on a hot pad on your worktable.

Use the tip of a teaspoon to make a shallow groove along the top of each banana half. Fill each groove with honey. (About one-quarter teaspoon for each.) *Serves 4.*

Astroextra: This recipe is good to serve with Skywheel Omelet.

Astrotwister: Say Bramble berry breakfast five times fast.

Astrojoke:
First astrocook, yawning, "Do you ever wake up grumpy in the morning?"
Second astrocook, "Never! I let the Commander sleep as long as possible. Even if I have to hold breakfast."

☆ SUNNYSIDE GRAPEFRUIT

These grapefruit halves are as sunny-bright as the side of Mercury that faces the sun.

2 grapefruits	*paring knife*
¼ cup honey	*cutting board*
4 strawberries (optional)	*measuring cup and spoons*

Place grapefruit on cutting board and slice in half with paring knife. Be sure to cut half-way between the blossom end and stem end, like this.

Poke out any seeds, then use the knife to cut carefully along the edge of each section so the fruit will be easy to remove with a spoon. Cut out the white core. Pour tablespoon of honey into each half. Top with one plump strawberry, if berries are in season. Cover tightly with plastic wrap or with foil and chill in refrigerator until crew comes for breakfast. *Serves 4.*

Astroextra: This recipe is good to serve with Weightless Pancakes.

Astrofact: Because the sun doesn't move in orbit as the planets do, early scientists thought it always stayed in the same place. But now we know the sun is moving steadily (at about 12 miles an hour) toward the constellation (or group of stars) known as Hercules. And of course the planets are moving with the sun. This means the planets move three ways. They are spinning and orbiting and moving toward a distant group of stars—all at once!

SUN PUZZLE

Across:

   4. Nine of them orbit our sun.
   6. A sun is also called a _____.
   7. To see the stars, you must look where?
   9. One of the gasses inside a star.
   10. Where is the sun located in our solar system?

Down:

   1. The sun and planets together are called a _____. (two words)
   2. Never look directly at the _____.
   3. Stars are made of _____.
   5. Another word for rotate.
   8. Earth's loop around the sun is called an _____.

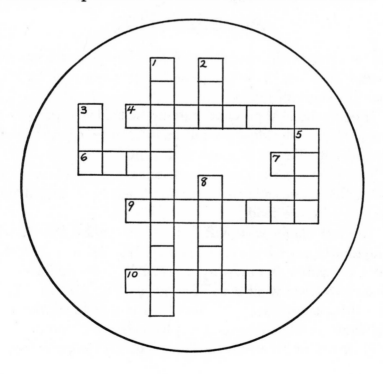

MERCURY MUNCHIES
Appetizers

Appetizer Hog

The extra-credit class tour of far planets was going fine except for Greg. At every planet stop, Greg took far more than his share of food.

"Food's the best part of the tour," he said when the others complained. "Besides, my folks paid plenty for me to come on this trip. I'll eat as much as I want."

The others were embarrassed, but Greg didn't care. "I'm doing the natives a favor," he said. "Next time, they'll know they need more food."

The last planet was Wiff, in the fifth galaxy from Earth. The tour teacher was excited about Wiff. Her eyes sparkled. "We know there's a mystery," she said. "Now we'll have the chance to learn what it is." She gave Greg a frown. "You'll like this planet, Greg. Wiffian food is said to be the most delicious in the universe. But please try to be polite."

"Just tell us about the mystery," he said impatiently.

"It has something to do with the food," she said. "But no one seems to know. Very few explorers have come out this far. We are lucky to have been accepted for a visit."

Greg wasn't listening. He was thinking of the food. He could hardly wait for planet fall.

The class was barely off the ship when Wiffians arrived with appetizer Planetrays.

"The food is great," Greg said with his mouth full. He grabbed another handful from a passing tray and stuffed it in his mouth. "Where's the mystery?"

The teacher frowned. "Do try to be polite, Greg."

A Wiffian came in suddenly. "Welcome to Wiff," he said. "You may have heard our food is praised throughout the universe. Now you will know the rumors are true."

Greg stuffed the last appetizer in his mouth and looked around, eager for this great food. But the Wiffian was still talking.

"On Wiff we believe the guest should have the food he deserves. Because of this, most of our guests leave saying they have eaten the most delicious food in the universe."

He waved his hand. A green haze settled over the room. "However," the Wiffian said, "a few adjustments are necessary."

Greg stared around him. His classmates were growing wings right before his eyes. One by one they followed their host to the top of fruit-laden trees.

They seemed to be enjoying the fruit. Greg would never know how it tasted. For after the green haze made its change in him, he could only use his snout to root around in the Wiffian soil for roots and grubs.

Astrofact: Mercury, the smallest planet, moves fast and is even closer to the sun than the Earth is. Because of this we don't know much about Mercury. It's probably very hot on the side of Mercury that is facing the sun—

probably too hot to sustain any life. Like all planets, Mercury rotates (spins) as it revolves around (orbits) the sun. No moons orbit Mercury.

☆ BUG-EYED MONSTERS

Your astroguests can create their own funny good-tasing "monsters."

6 eggs
1 tbsp Worcestershire
  sauce
½ tsp salt
¼ tsp pepper
1 tsp prepared mustard
2 tbsp mayonnaise
face makings—sprigs of
  parsley, bits of
  pimento, rings and
  chunks of black or
  green olives, chopped
  pickle, paprika, or
  other toppings.

saucepan with lid
fork
mixing bowl
measuring spoons
paring knife
cutting board
serving plates
serving tray for toppings

To hard-cook eggs, place them in saucepan, cover with cold water, and put lid on pan. Place over medium heat and bring to a boil. Turn off heat. Leave eggs in covered pan for 25 minutes.

Peel cooled eggs. Cut them in half lengthwise. Carefully pop the yolks into a mixing bowl and mash them thoroughly with a fork. Then mix in the Worcestershire sauce, salt, pepper, and mustard. Stir in enough mayonnaise to moisten the mixture so it holds together. Use a teaspoon to mound the yolk mixture into the egg white halves. Chill in refrigerator. Serve each guest one or two stuffed eggs and offer a choice of face makers.

Poke in a sprig of parsley for hair; sprinkle with paprika to turn the yolk face red; add bits and chunks of other toppings to make eyes, mouth, whatever appeals to you. *Makes 12 Bug-eyed Monsters.*

Astroextra: Bug-eyed Monsters make a good salad, too. Serve on a lettuce leaf with a slice of tomato.

Astroriddle: When you buy a dozen Mercury eggs for boiling, how can you be sure there are no baby lizards inside? *Buy Mercury duck eggs.*

☆ BLACK HOLES

In the astrocook's kitchen, Black Holes are ripe black olives with sizzling cheese centers, wrapped in bacon.

1 can pitted ripe olives	*paring knife*
sharp cheddar cheese	*cutting board*
bacon	*tongs*
	paper towels
	plate
	shallow baking pan
	potholders or mitt

Cut cheese into cubes just big enough to stuff into the olives. Cut bacon strips into two-inch long pieces, one for each cheese-stuffed olive. Wrap the bacon around the olives and fasten with toothpicks. Turn oven on to "Broil." Place Black Holes in shallow baking pan, slide under broiler, and cook until bacon is crisp. Turn off oven.

Fold paper towels into three or four layers. Place them on serving plate. With potholders or mitts, remove tray from broiler. Use tongs to lift Black Holes onto paper towels to drain. (Hot bacon grease burns—young astrocooks should ask an adult to help remove the pan from the broiler and drain it.)

Astrofact: In space, black holes are collapsed stars with such dense gravity not even light can escape from them.

☆ SOLAR HALOS

Never look directly at the sun; but you can see Solar Halos after you prepare these appetizers.

1 unsplit sandwich roll or bun	*saucepan or broiler*
	fork
1 hot dog	*table knife*
prepared mustard	*cutting board*
pickle relish (optional)	*spoon*

Boil or broil the hot dog. Remove from heat and set aside. Cut thin slice from each end of sandwich roll. Use a fork to hollow out the center so you can push a hot dog through. (Save crumbs for topping next time you have a casserole.) Spread the inside of the roll with mustard. Push in the

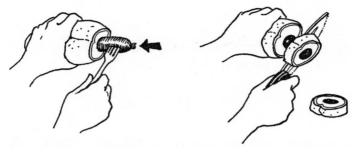

cooked hot dog. Wrap the roll in waxed paper and chill. When ready to serve, cut into slices about one-inch thick. Dot each slice with a bit of pickle relish if you like it. *Makes 6 slices.*

Astroextra: To serve Solar Halos warm, use a small fold of waxed paper to grease a cookie sheet with butter or margarine. Turn oven to 400 degrees. Place Solar Halos on cookie sheet. If you like, add a small chunk of cheese, placing it on top of the hot dog slice. Cook under the broiler until lightly browned.

Astrotwister: Say this seven times speedily: Solar Halos surely are scrumptious.

MERCURY DIPS

These two dips are good with carrot sticks, celery strips, zucchini slices, crackers, and chips.

☆ DAY-SIDE DIP

(The temperature on the sunny side of Mercury is about 700 degrees!)

1 8-oz can refried beans	*small saucepan*
¼ cup grated cheese	*grater*
½ tsp onion powder	*mixing spoon*
½ tsp garlic powder	*can opener*
2 tbsp taco sauce	

Mix all ingredients in saucepan. Heat slowly (do not boil) until cheese is melted. Serve warm.

☆ NIGHT-SIDE DIP

(The temperature on the night side of Mercury drops to about 400 degrees below zero!)

1 ripe avocado	*mixing bowl and small bowl*
1 cup sour cream	*fork*
1 tsp lemon juice	*rubber spatula*

Peel avocado, remove pit, and mash the fruit in a bowl. Stir in sour cream and lemon juice and mix well. Use rubber spatula to scrape mixture out of mixing bowl into smaller serving bowl. Cover with a lid or foil or plastic wrap. Chill in the refrigerator for 15 minutes or more before serving.

Astrofact: When Mariner 10 photos of the planet Mercury are placed beside photos of Earth's moon and the planet Mars, the cratered surfaces in all the photos look very much alike.

☆☆☆ STAR PUFFS

When you're having an astrocrowd over, offer them these sandwich-style cream puffs.

1 cup water	*saucepan*
½ cup butter or margarine	*measuring cup and spoon*
½ tsp salt	*mixing spoon*
1 cup flour	*cookie sheet*
4 eggs at room temperature	*potholders or mitts*
	waxed paper
	paring knife

Take eggs from refrigerator about an hour before you are ready to cook. Place them in a bowl (so they won't roll) on the counter to warm up.

Put water, butter, and salt in the saucepan. Heat until butter melts. Add the flour all at once and stir quickly with a wooden mixing spoon, until the dough pulls away from the pan and makes a ball. Turn off the heat. Use a potholder to take the pan to your worktable. Beat in the eggs, one at a time, with the mixing spoon.

Turn oven to 375 degrees. With a fold of waxed paper, rub butter or margarine over a cookie sheet. Use a teaspoon to drop small spoonfuls of dough onto the sheet. Bake for 45 minutes until dough swells up and becomes puffy and dry. Use potholder or mitt to take sheet to worktable. (Protect it with hot pads before you set the sheet down.)

With a paring knife, cut slits in the shells so they will dry inside. Fill with sandwich mixtures. *Serves 10 or more.*

Sandwich Mixtures: Blend deviled ham with just enough mayonnaise to moisten. Add chopped pickle if you like.

Blend tuna with enough mayonnaise to moisten. Add 1 tablespoon finely chopped onion if you like.

Puff in a filling of cheese spread.

Astroriddle: Bob and Jim held a contest to see who could eat the most Star Puffs in an hour. Bob ate 99, but Jim beat him. How many Star Puffs did Jim eat? *He ate a hundred and won.*

Astrofact: Some scientists believe that Mercury was once a satellite of the planet Venus.

Astrotwister: Say this five times fast: Mercury monsters munch meteors merrily.

☆ PLANETRAY

This attractive appetizer plate represents the sun and the nine surrounding planets.

cottage cheese	*large spoon*
paprika	*can opener for olives*
large lettuce leaf	*paring knife*
carrots	*vegetable peeler*
cauliflower	*vegetable brush*
celery	*large dinner plate or*
radishes	*serving platter*
green onions	
tomatoes	
olives	
zucchini squash	
crackers	

Place lettuce leaf in center of plate. Using a large spoon, make a mound of cottage cheese on the lettuce. Sprinkle lightly with paprika. Surround the cottage cheese with seven sections of vegetables, one of crackers, one of olives.

To prepare vegetables: scrub carrots with brush, cut into strips. Cut stem from cauliflower, break the head into flowerets, wash. Wash celery, cut off leaves (save them for green salad), run vegetable peeler along the back of celery stalk to remove strings. Cut top and root from radishes, wash. Cut tip from the root end of green onions, wash, pull off any wilted leaves. Leave skins on tomatoes, cut out blossom end, cut in quarters. Or use cherry tomatoes. Scrub zucchini with vegetable brush but do not peel. Slice in thin rounds.

Invite astrocrew to dip raw vegetables into cottage cheese and eat. *Serves 10 or more.*

Astrojoke:

First astrocook: "Did you hear the story about the empty planetray?"

Second astrocook: "No."

First astrocook: "It doesn't matter. There was nothing in it anyway."

☆ SPACE TUGS

Scientists are planning ways to build space tugs for solar travel. They will transport people and cargo, using moon debris for fuel. You might imagine what they will look like while you prepare this recipe.

2 small cucumbers
peanut butter

paring knife
vegetable peeler
table knife

Peel cucumbers and split in half lengthwise. Scrape out seeds and the pulpy material surrounding them. Using a table knife, spread a thin layer of peanut butter over the hollow of each cucumber half. Serve on lettuce leaves. *Serves 4.*

Astroriddle: When do astrocooks have six arms? *When there are three of them.*

☆ COSMIC STRIPS

Cosmic rays contain protons and electrons. In this recipe perhaps the brown strips represent protons, the white, electrons.

celery	*vegetable peeler*
peanut butter	*paring knife*
cream cheese	*table knife*

Allow two pieces of celery for each guest. (And two for yourself.) Scrub celery stalks. Cut off leaves. (Save for salad.) Run the vegetable peeler along the back of each celery stalk to remove the strings. Leave short stalks whole. Cut long stalks in half crosswise. Use table knife to fill half the celery stalks with peanut butter. Fill the rest with cream cheese. Or if you prefer, fill one end of each stalk with peanut butter and the other end with cream cheese.

Astrofact: A meteoroid is a chunk of iron or rock, possibly broken from an asteroid. If it falls into Earth's atmosphere, it becomes a meteor and is usually burned by friction. If it does not burn and it falls to Earth, it is called a meteorite.

☆☆ CHEESE METEORS

Cheese Meteors disappear as fast as the real thing when your crew tastes them.

1 cup flour	*sifter*
1½ tsp baking powder	*bowl*
½ tsp salt	*measuring cup and spoons*
2 tbsp butter or margarine	*pastry blender or*
½ cup grated Cheddar	*two knives*
cheese	*fork*
⅓ cup cold water	*pastry board*
	rolling pin
	1-inch canape or
	biscuit cutter

Sift flour, baking powder, and salt into medium-size bowl. Add grated cheese and butter or margarine. Cut into flour mixture with pastry blender or two knives. (With knives, take one in each hand, crisscross them so each points to the opposite side of the bowl, cut toward and past each other. Repeat many times until mixture is blended and crumbly.) Sprinkle cold water over mixture. Mix lightly with fork until dough sticks together and leaves the sides of the bowl.

Roll dough into a twelve-inch wide round on a floured pastry board. Use a one-inch canape cutter to cut rounds and other shapes. Put onto ungreased cookie sheet. (Tear odd-shaped trimmings into two-inch lengths and put on another cookie sheet to bake into space "debris.")

Bake at 425 degrees for 10 minutes, or until light brown. Cool on wire racks. *Serves 6 or more.*

Astroriddle: What's flecked with orange, goes fast, and tastes good? *A Cheese Meteor.*

MERCURY PUZZLE

Across:

4. Mercury orbits what solar body?
5. Mercury is the planet _____ to the sun.
6. What planet is the seventh from the sun?
8. What do we call chunks of rock that enter Earth's atmosphere and burn?
9. Black holes may be collapsed _____.
10. Name of mission that took our first photos of Mercury.

Down:

1. Mercury was named for the Roman god of speed. Its orbit is _____.
2. Mercury's surface temperature is _____.
3. Some believe Mercury was once a satellite of what planet?
5. What surface feature do photos show on Mercury, Mars, and Earth's moon?
7. An astrocook is also called a _____ cook.
11. How many moons orbit Mercury?

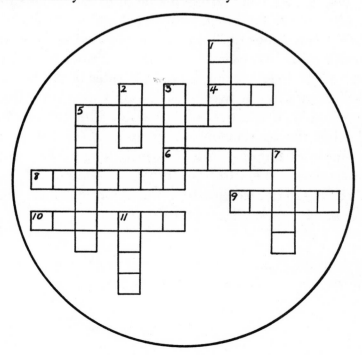

VENUS VITTLES
Main Dishes

The Perfect Space Lab Loaf

Brill was the best and most creative cook in the Venusian colony. But he was not the best-liked.

For one thing, Brill kept all the most interesting recipes for himself and left the two assistant cooks the easy and ordinary ones. Worse yet, Brill was more interested in creative cooking than in serving the crew.

"Fancy is fine, Brill," the colony leader kept saying. "But the crew likes Skywheel Omelets served hot and Super Green Spaceship Supreme served cold. Most of all, they want their food served *on time*."

Brill smiled and nodded, but it was clear he wasn't listening. He went on making his recipes more and more carefully and slowly. They were culinary masterpieces when they were finished, but by then the crew was too hungry to care.

When galactic guests came for dinner, the colony kitchen buzzed with excitement.

"Remember, Brill," the leader warned again. "Fancy food is nice, but good food served on time is best!"

Brill smiled, nodded his head, and hummed to himself while he turned to his fancy recipes cooking tape.

He decided to make a meat loaf shaped like a space lab with vegetables cupped in each of the end caps. It would be perfect, he thought happily. Visitors could nibble appetizers if they must. Good food took time.

When the dinner hour grew near, the two assistant cooks hurried about preparing the other foods. They frowned with worry when they saw Brill tinting mashed potatoes blue with food coloring. They worried more when they saw him carefully shaping and reshaping the meat loaf. "It's going to be perfect," they heard him say.

The galactic guests finished their appetizers, their salad, and even their Zoom Soup. They were ready for the Space Lab Loaf.

But Brill the cook was not ready for them. He was carefully decorating the Space Lab Loaf so it would look perfectly real.

Finally, the leader whispered to the assistant cooks. They rushed to broil hamburgers and cook quick vegetables for the hungry guests.

It was a good meal, but not a fancy one.

When the guests had gone, Brill rushed from the kitchen with a smile as big as a sun on his face. "It's finished," he cried. "It's perfect. It's so real, it could fly." Then he looked back into the kitchen and screamed.

The perfect Space Lab Loaf had lifted from the blue mashed potato sky and was whirring straight toward his head.

Astrofact: Venus, our twin planet (almost the same size as Earth), orbits the sun in 225 days; so a year on Venus is shorter than a year on Earth.

Astroriddle: What time is it when the space lab crew gets hungry? *Time to serve them Space Lab Loaf.*

☆☆☆ SPACE LAB LOAF

Most people prefer their potatoes white, not blue, but you can make Brill's Space Lab Loaf for your next dinner party.

1½ lbs ground beef
½ lb ground pork
2 cups dry bread crumbs
2 eggs
1 14½-oz can evaporated
  milk
2 tsp onion powder
2 tsp salt
2 tbsp Worcestershire
  sauce
4 cups mashed potatoes
canned or frozen
  vegetables
raw carrots
Comet Tail Sauce
  (Chapter 5) or gravy
  made from package mix

measuring spoons
measuring cups
bowl
baking pan
mixing spoon
fork
spatula
saucepans
paring knife
cutting board
potholders or mitt
large tray or serving
  platter

Put first eight ingredients into a large bowl. With clean hands (and fingernails) mix everything together until blended. Shape about one cup of the mixture into a large round and place it in your baking pan. Mash down the center and build up the sides to make a bowl shape. Take a smaller amount of mixture (about one-half cup) and shape into smaller rounds with hollow middles. You should have

one large round and at least six smaller ones. Turn oven on to 350 degrees, but don't start baking yet.

Following recipe for mashed potatoes in Chapter 5, put water on to boil and peel and cut up potatoes. Add potatoes to boiling water. Now put Space Lab Loaves in oven and bake for 30 minutes while preparing the rest of the meal.

Prepare Comet Tail Sauce (Chapter 5) or gravy from a package mix. Set aside.

After loaves have been baking for 15 minutes, prepare frozen vegetables following package directions. Or if canned vegetables are to be used, allow loaves to bake for 25 minutes, then prepare as follows: pour liquid from canned vegetables into saucepan. Cover with lid and heat over medium heat until liquid just begins to simmer. Add vegetables, cover with lid, and heat two minutes more.

When canned or frozen vegetables are ready, turn off heat and leave on stove, with the lid on the pan, while mashing potatoes. Then place Comet Tail Sauce or gravy over low heat while assembling Space Lab Loaf as follows:

Spread mashed potatoes over a large tray. Use a spatula to lift the large meatloaf to the center of the tray. Place smaller meat rounds in a circle around the large one, but not touching it. Poke raw carrot sticks between each smaller round and its neighbor so that all parts of the Space Lab Loaf are connected. Spoon cooked vegetables into each of the smaller rounds. If using gravy, pour into the mound on top of large loaf. Serve Comet Tail Sauce (or extra gravy) in a side dish. *Serves 8 to 10.*

Astrofact: Skylab, an orbiting workshop, was launched by the United States on May 14, 1973. The crew spent 28 days in orbit. The second Skylab team orbited Earth for 59 days before returning. The third Skylab crew worked, slept, ate, studied, and exercised in space for 84 days—almost three months. Fears that Skylab would fall from orbit and burn up in Earth's atmosphere caused a "Save Skylab" mission. A remote-control add-on rocket will propel Skylab into a higher orbit or, if necessary, destroy it away from populated areas.

Astroriddle: What would happen if your Venusian dinner wiggled free of your fork and dropped into the sea? *It would get wet.*

Astrofact: Venus is called Earth's twin—not because it looks like Earth, but because it is approximately the same size.

An odyssey is a long journey, and that's what a trip to Venus would be. Before you leave, better fill up with this easy dinner.

6 cups water	*small bowl*
1 cup macaroni	*large saucepan*
1 tbsp vegetable oil	*small saucepan with lid*
½ cup milk	*measuring cup*
½ lb Cheddar cheese	*cheese grater*
butter or margarine	*casserole dish*
	waxed paper

Turn oven to 350 degrees. Using a fold of wax paper, rub margarine around inside of casserole dish and set aside. Pour six cups of water and tablespoon of oil in large saucepan. Cover and bring to a boil. Remove lid and set it aside. Carefully drop macaroni into boiling water. Cook, stirring occasionally, until tender. (Approximately 7 minutes.) While macaroni cooks, grate cheese. (Always push cheese away from yourself with grater aimed toward bowl. Keep your fingers away from the sharp grater edges.)

When macaroni is tender, drain off boiling water. (Young astrocooks should ask an adult to help.) Place macaroni in greased casserole. Heat milk in small saucepan over low heat, but do not boil. When the first small bubble forms where the milk touches the edge of the pan, add the cheese. Continue heating and stir until cheese has melted. Slowly pour milk and cheese over macaroni. Mix with spoon. Bake without a lid at 350 degrees for 20 minutes. *Serves 4.*

Astroriddle: What stays hot longest in the astrocook's refrigerator? *Pepper.*

Astrofact: We don't know what Venus looks like because it is hidden under an atmosphere too thick to see through. But space explorers have used instruments to tell us that the temperature on Venus is about 800 degrees. Radar indicates Venusian mountains, craters, peaks, moonlike basins, a canyon, and a huge volcanic peak, but no oceans.

☆ VENUS VITTLES

This is as mysterious as the second planet. You don't have to tell anyone what's in this recipe. Just let them guess why it tastes so good.

1 6½-oz can tuna	*medium saucepan with lid*
1 8-oz can peas	*mixing spoon*
1 10¾-oz can cream of	*measuring cup*
chicken soup	*cutting board*
⅓ cup powdered milk	*paring knife*
three slices bread	

Drain liquid from tuna. Place tuna in saucepan. Add soup. Pour powdered milk into measuring cup. Into the same cup, drain the liquid from the can of peas and mix well. Add peas to soup and tuna, pour in the milk mixture, and stir until ingredients are well mixed. Heat over low flame, stirring occasionally. Do not boil.

When mixture is hot, turn off heat, and cover pan with a lid while you toast the bread. Cut toast in quarters, cutting from corner to corner. This makes twelve toast diamonds.

Place three diamonds on each plate, and top with Venus Vittle mix. *Serves 4.*

41

Astrojoke:

Big brother: What are you drawing?
Little Brother: A picture of planet Venus.
Big brother: But nobody knows what Venus looks like.
Little Brother: They will when I finish my picture.

Astrofact: A satellite is a smaller body, orbiting a larger one. The moon is Earth's natural satellite. Artificial satellites have been constructed on Earth and launched into orbit to help us learn more about our universe.

☆☆ SATELLITE SUPPER I

Satellites come in all sizes. This recipe makes large ones with a delightful pizza flavor.

1 large round loaf French bread	*cheese grater*
butter or margarine	*saucepan*
1 8-oz can tomato sauce	*mixing spoon*
1 can water	*table knife*
2 tbsp onion flakes	*measuring spoons*
1 tsp oregano	*cookie sheet*
dash of salt and pepper	*potholders or mitts*
½ lb Monterey Jack cheese	*waxed paper*

With a small fold of waxed paper, grease cookie sheet with margarine and set aside. Grate cheese and set aside. Pour tomato sauce into saucepan. Fill tomato-sauce can with water and add water to sauce in pan. Also add onion flakes, oregano, salt, and pepper. Stir well. Place pan on stove over medium heat. Stir now and then until mixture just begins to simmer. Do not boil.

While tomato mixture is heating, turn oven to 400 de

42

grees. Split French bread in half this way --(------)-
to make two circles.

Spread bread lightly with butter or margarine. Toast under broiler until lightly browned and crisped. Remove bread from broiler, using potholders or mitts, and turn oven down to 350 degrees.

Place toasted bread circles on greased cookie sheet. Pour half the tomato sauce over first circle. Pour remaining sauce mix over the second circle. Sprinkle each circle with cheese. Place satellites in oven and bake 15 to 20 minutes. *Serves 6.*

Astroextra: You can add other ingredients to one or both of your satellites just before baking. For one circle top with ¼ cup of chopped olives, chopped green peppers, hamburger (fried and crumbled), or chopped leftover chicken.

☆☆ SATELLITE SUPPER II— THE SMALL ONE

A small satellite pizza for each of your crew is easy to make. Be ready if they ask for more!

3 English muffins, cut in half
¼ cup vegetable oil
1 10-oz can pizza sauce
dried oregano
1 8-oz package sliced American cheese
1 4½-oz can sliced black olives
1 4-oz can sliced mushrooms
any other pizza topping you like

cookie sheet
saucer
measuring cup
pastry brush
paring knife
cutting board
can opener
potholders or mitts

43

Turn oven to 400 degrees.

Place muffin halves on cookie sheet, cut side up. Pour oil into saucer. Use pastry brush to cover surface of each muffin with oil, then cover each with pizza sauce. Sprinkle on oregano—just a thumb and finger pinch for each. Add black olives, mushrooms, and any other pizza fixings you like. Put the tray of small satellites into a hot oven for 15 minutes.

While the satellites bake, cut the thin cheese slices into strips about one-half inch wide. When muffin edges are lightly browned (after about 15 minutes), use potholders or mitts to remove the tray and take it to your work surface. Place cheese strips over the satellites in spoke-fashion. Return the tray to the oven and bake 5 minutes more, until the cheese is melted. *Serves 3 to 6.*

Astroriddle: What did the satellite say to the salad? *Nothing. A satellite can't talk.*

☆☆ SKYWALK TRIO

One recipe to make three ways—the choice is yours.

1 cup macaroni *or* noodles *or* spaghetti	*cheese grater*
	large saucepan
1 tbsp vegetable oil	*small saucepan*
1 10-oz can enchilada sauce	*casserole dish*
	potholders or mitts
1 tbsp onion flakes	*waxed paper*
1 cup Monterey Jack cheese	
¼ cup sour cream	
1 8-oz can corn	

Using a small fold of waxed paper, grease the inside of a casserole dish and set aside. Grate cheese and set aside. In

44

large saucepan bring six cups of water to boil and add table-spoon of oil. Carefully drop in macaroni, noodles, or spaghetti, a little at a time. Stir and cook until tender. (About 7 minutes.) Drain off boiling water. (Younger cooks should ask for help with this.)

Pour macaroni, noodles, or spaghetti into greased casserole. In small saucepan, heat enchilada sauce, but do not boil. Add cheese and onion flakes, stir, and heat 2 minutes. Turn off heat. Now add sour cream. Drain liquid from can of corn, add corn to mixture in saucepan, and stir well. Pour sauce over macaroni, noodles, or spaghetti and stir until well mixed.

Bake without a lid at 350 degrees for 20 minutes. *Serves 4.*

Astroriddles: What kind of moon is like yeast dough? *Moon-rise.*

What kind of moon was against the law during Prohibition on Earth? *Moonshine.*

What do you call a sidewalk outside your lunar dome? *Moonwalk.*

What kind of moon has no gravity? *Moonlight.*

What do lunar astrocooks use to hold up their kitchen roofs? *Moonbeams.*

Astroriddle: What goes clomp, clomp, clomp, clomp, clomp, clomp, clomp, squish? *An eight-legged Venusian cook with one wet shoe.*

☆☆☆ SLOPPY JOE VOLCANOES

You wouldn't want to eat a Volcano for every meal, but it's a great treat when you have time to make a very special dinner.

1½ cups Quick Brown Rice	*dry cup measure*
1 lb hamburger	*liquid cup measure*
½ cup chopped onion	*measuring spoons*
1 tbsp butter or margarine	*deep saucepan with lid*
1 tsp salt	*mixing spoon*
¼ tsp pepper	*table knife*
1 2-oz can sliced	*paring knife*
mushrooms	*cutting board*
1 8-oz can tomato sauce	*can opener*
2 tbsp vinegar	*skillet*
1 tbsp cornstarch	*custard cup*
½ cup beef broth	*individual serving plate*
vegetable oil	

Follow package directions to steam rice. While rice is cooking, melt butter or margarine in skillet. Crumble hamburger into skillet, add chopped onions, and fry until meat is brown, while continuing to stir and break up meat. Add salt, pepper, undrained mushrooms, tomato sauce, and vinegar. Cook together over medium heat. Measure broth from tin or use powdered broth mix to make on-half cup. Stir in cornstarch, then add mixture to hamburger mix. Cook, stirring, until mixture boils. Keep warm.

Oil a custard cup or other cup-size container with sloped sides. Use tablespoon to pack cooked rice into cup, then turn out on individual serving plate. With the spoon carefully push a hollow into the top. Repeat with remaining rice. Spoon hamburger mix into and over the volcanoes and serve. *Makes 6 volcanoes.*

Astrotwister: Say this fast as many times as you can. Earth's creatures eat Venus Vittles.

Astrofact: Sunrise and sunset are especially spectacular on Venus because of the thick gaseous clouds (mostly carbon dioxide) which surround the planet. Like Mercury and Earth, Venus has an iron-rich core.

☆☆ SEA CREATURE PIE

When it stops wriggling, it's ready to eat.

1 9-inch pie shell	*strainer*
1 9-oz can tuna	*grater*
¼ lb Swiss cheese	*paring knife*
¼ cup grated Parmesan	*cutting board*
cheese	*bowl*
2 green onions, with tops	*eggbeater or wire whip*
3 eggs	*potholders or mitts*
1 cup milk	
½ tsp salt	
¼ tsp nutmeg	
⅛ tsp pepper	

Make a pie shell as directed for Applesaucers (Chapter 9), or buy one ready-made. Bake according to directions and set aside.

Drain tuna in strainer, then scatter tuna over bottom of pie shell. Grate Swiss cheese (slant grater into a bowl, remembering to keep your fingers away from the sharp edges). Sprinkle Swiss cheese over the tuna. Chop the green onions and tops to make one-quarter cup. Sprinkle the onions and Parmesan cheese over the Swiss cheese and tuna. Beat the eggs in a bowl, then beat in the milk, salt, nutmeg, and pepper. Pour the egg and milk mixture over the tuna and cheese. Turn oven to 350 degrees. Bake Sea Creature Pie for about 45 minutes. Test for doneness by using potholders or mitts to shake the dish gently. The middle should stay firm. Remove from oven and let set for 10 minutes before serving. *Serves 6.*

Astroriddle: What has 6 legs, 2 arms, 3 heads, and 2 tails? *An Earthling on horseback bringing home a tuna fish.*

☆☆ STAR-STUDDED HAM

Beginning cooks can star-stud a ham for an adult who takes the hot dish in and out of the oven. Older astrocooks can cook the ham themselves, or try this recipe with a thick ham slice. Fasten the stars along the sides.

1 ham or ham slice	*star-shaped canape cutter*
1 cup honey	*measuring cup*
2 large oranges	*paring knife*
4 slices pineapple	*cutting board*
whole cloves	*baking dish*
	potholders or mitts
	large spoon
	bowl
	skewer
	fork

Set oven at 325 degrees. Place ham in baking dish. Follow cooking time on wrapper or can. One hour before ham is done, use potholders or mitts to remove from oven. Use knife to cut through the ham fat, making slits to shape large squares. Pour one-half cup honey over top of ham. Return it to the oven, bake another 30 minutes until honey is shiny and lightly browned.

Wash the oranges. Use the paring knife to cut through the rind of each orange, top to bottom, in four sections. Remove the rind and use canape cutter to punch out stars. Scrape away as much of the white inner layer as possible. Set stars aside.

Break oranges into sections. Pull away white fibers. Cut pineapple slices in half. Remove ham from oven. Place orange peel stars, orange sections, and pineapple around ham in the pan. Drizzle remaining honey over them. Return to oven. Bake 20 minutes until the fruit is shiny and the peel is tender.

Remove from oven. Use skewer to poke a small hole through each star. (Handle stars with a fork—they're hot.) Put a whole clove through each hole. Poke one clove-star into each fat square on the ham. Use a spoon to dip honey and fruit syrup from the pan and drizzle it over the top of the ham. Heat for 10 minutes. Before serving, remove ham to platter. (Younger cooks should ask an adult to help.) Place glazed (shiny) fruit around the edges.

Astroextra: Make orange peel stars anytime. Put in small greased baking dish. Spread with honey. Bake 20 minutes at 325 degrees. Skewer and stud with cloves as above. Then drop stars into hot cocoa or Dark-Side Punch.

VENUS PUZZLE

Across:

3. Skylab is the name given to an orbiting
_____ launched by the U. S.
4. Is air pressure on Venus low or high?
6. Venus is the _____ planet from the sun.
9. Do we expect to find our kind of life on Venus?
10. Number of oceans seen on Venus.

Down:

1. Because of its size, Venus is sometimes called
_____. (two words)
2. Venus's surface temperature is _____.
5. The core of Venus is thought to be rich in what metal?
7. Venus is covered by thick _____.
8. Gaseous clouds surrounding Venus are mostly carbon
_____.

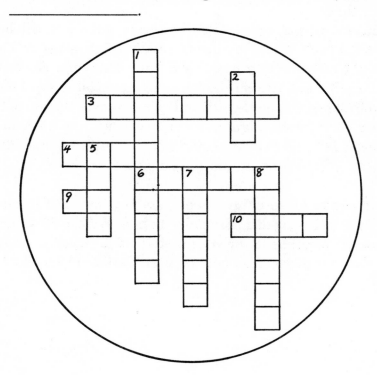

EARTH EXTRAS
Vegetables

Trick or Trap?

Trudging through the cornfield, Duke shivered as a dark cloud scuttled across the moon. Ghostly light filtered through, turning cornstalks into witches. Writhing in the wind, they clutched at Duke with raspy arms. They whispered and cackled behind his back.

He shivered again, remembering how this dare had started. He had been walking home from the Halloween party, telling Bill and Will about the joke he had pulled on little Jimmy last year.

"I've pulled a lot of tricks on that little kid," Duke grinned. "But never one as good as that one!"

"How come?" asked Bill.

"Oh—ho—ho—I told him—" Duke laughed so hard he could hardly talk. "Told him—on Halloween—a tiny mean man from Mars would be hiding inside a pumpkin in the cornfield. Bet him two dozen donuts he'd be scared to stay out there till midnight."

"Jimmy loves donuts," Will murmured. "Was he scared?"

"Was he?" Duke roared. "I had this microphone set up, see? Made it sound like Martian talk coming from the pumpkin. You should have seen that dummy run. It took all his lunch money for two weeks, but I got my donuts all right."

"You won't believe this," said Will. "But tonight there really is a visitor from outer space hanging around our cornfield."

"Yeah," said Bill. "It's the scarecrow. Three dozen donuts says you can't stay out there with him until midnight."

Duke had laughed then, but now, alone in the cornfield, he wasn't even smiling. He was close enough to see the scarecrow. Arms outstretched, head bowed, gloved hands waggling, it shuddered in every blast of wind.

"Pssst!"

What was that! A cornstalk rattling? No. It must have been the scarecrow.

"Some joke." Duke looked around for the microphone. "Those guys can't scare me with my own trick."

"Come closer," the scarecrow whispered. "Take my hat and put it on."

Duke grabbed the ragged hat. Looking around for Bill and Will, he jammed the dusty thing on his head.

"Gloves," the scarecrow whispered. "Take the gloves and wear them."

Duke pulled on the dirty gloves and felt goose bumps trickle down his arms.

"Quick!" The scarecrow's voice was stronger. "Pull the broomstick out of my sleeves. Hurry!"

Duke clutched the stick. His body stiffened. His arms stretched straight out from his shoulders. He couldn't bend them. His head dropped. He couldn't lift it. He couldn't see.

But he could feel the icy wind. And he could hear footsteps rustling away through the cornstalks. And a strange voice calling back.

"Thanks! The spacecraft captain said if I could trick an Earthling—before midnight—I could take his place on this planet. Bill and Will were too smart for me. But they were kind enough to help."

Too late the new scarecrow remembered—Bill and Will were little Jimmy's brothers.

Astrofact: Earth is a middle-size planet that rotates once every 24 hours. (So on Earth, one day and night together is 24 hours.) Earth orbits the sun once every 365 days. (So on Earth, one year is 365 days.) Earth has one satellite known as the moon. Both are in the milky way galaxy.

Astrotwister: This is just a tiny tongue twister. Say it ten times fast. Earth's easy extras.

☆ STAR STUFFS

Star-shaped bread cups hold your favorite creamed vegetable for a side-dish satellite.

4 slices of bread	*hot pad*
1 1-lb 1-oz can cream-style	*paring knife*
vegetables	*cutting board*
butter or margarine	*table knife*
	muffin pan
	small covered saucepan
	fork
	potholders or mitts
	4 serving dishes

Turn oven on to 400 degrees.

Using cutting board and paring knife, cut crusts from bread, close to the edge. Spread butter or margarine lightly over both sides of each slice, then press one slice into each of four muffin cups. (If your muffin pan has more than four cups, add water to cover the bottom of each empty cup to keep it from burning.)

Bake at 400 degrees for about 15 minutes, or until bread is crisp and lightly browned.

While Star cups are baking, prepare Stuffs—heat creamed vegetables in covered saucepan.

Use potholders or mitts to remove Star cups from oven. Place muffin pan on hot pad. Use fork to lift Star cups from muffin pan into serving plate, then spoon vegetables into each Star cup. *Serves 4.*

Astrofact: Comets called "sun grazers" make part of their orbits quite close to the sun. Sometimes they even pass through the sun's outer atmosphere.

☆ COMET TAIL SAUCE

Olive sauce as zippy as a comet tail adds flavor to cooked green beans and other vegetables.

½ cup ripe olives
¾ cup sour cream
1 tsp onion powder
1½ tsp lemon juice
½ tsp dry mustard
dash garlic powder
dash salt
dash pepper

can opener
measuring cup
measuring spoons
mixing spoon
small saucepan

Place olives in saucepan and crush with the back of a spoon so they break into large chunks. Add all other ingredients (A dash is less than a pinch. Just give the spice a quick shake over the top of the saucepan.) Mix well.

Place over medium heat and stir once in a while until sauce is heated through. Do not boil. When hot, pour over cooked green beans or other vegetables. Or serve in a side dish so your crew may add their own. *Serves 6.*

Astroknock Knock: Who's there? Comet. Comet who? Comet get it, supper's ready!

Astrofact: Scientists haven't discovered why a star will sometimes explode, but one that does is called a supernova.

☆☆ SUPERNOVA SPUDS

Why not serve exploded potatoes to your crew?

four medium potatoes
about ⅓ cup milk
1 tbsp butter or margarine
salt and pepper
paprika

vegetable brush
fork
medium bowl
measuring cups and spoons
knife
potholders or mitts
potato masher
baking pan or ovenproof
  serving dish

Turn oven on to 400 degrees. Scrub potatoes, then prick each one once with a fork. Carefully place potatoes in heated oven and bake about one hour or until tender when tested with a fork.

Using potholders or mitts, carefully remove potatoes from oven, but don't turn off the heat. Make a slit lengthwise along the top of each potato. Using the potholders, squeeze each potato gently so it will open without breaking the shell further.

Scoop out the fillings and place them in a mixing bowl. Add butter or margarine and enough milk to moisten potatoes, but not so much the mixture becomes soggy. Mash with potato masher until well mixed and fluffy. Sprinkle lightly with salt and pepper.

Loosely pile the potato mixture back into the shells. (Don't mash it down—it should be higher than the top of the shell, so it looks as if the potato has exploded.) Add a sprinkle of paprika to the potatoes and place them in a baking pan or ovenproof serving platter. Return to oven for about 10 minutes. Serve with butter, margarine, or sour cream and chives. *Serves 4.*

Astroriddle: What time is it when four Martian visitors on Earth divide one Supernova Spud? *Time to bake more, so every guest can have one.*

☆☆ ASTROMASHED POTATOES

The most nutritious mashed potatoes are cooked with their skins *on* and moistened with their own cooking water. Fortunately they also taste best when cooked this way.

2 cups water

5 medium potatoes

½ cup powdered milk

about ½ cup regular milk

½ tsp salt

2 tbsp butter or margarine

paring knife

vegetable brush

measuring cup and spoons

medium covered saucepan

fork

potato masher

potholders or mitts

hot pad

Astrotip: Start potatoes about 45 minutes before the rest of your meal will be ready.

Bring two cups of water to boil in covered saucepan. While water heats, scrub potatoes well with vegetable brush. Cut out any blemishes with paring knife, then cut each potato in half lengthwise. Carefully lower each half into boiling water. (Younger astrocooks should ask an adult to help.) Cover pan and simmer potatoes about 30 minutes, or until tender when tested with a fork.

Leave potatoes and cooking water in saucepan. Remove from stove and place pan on hot pad. Using a fork, break each potato half into small chunks. Add salt, butter or margarine, and powdered milk. Mash well with potato masher. If mixture is dry, add regular milk, about ¼ cup at a time, until the potatoes are moist enough to whip up smooth and creamy. Leave in pan with lid on to keep warm until ready to serve. *Serves 4.*

Astroriddle: What vegetable do astrocooks have the most trouble with? *Potatoes. They're always whipping, beating, or mashing them.*

THIS HURTS ME MORE THAN IT DOES YOU!

☆☆ ASTROMASHED PATTIES

Leftover mashed potatoes can be transformed into a delicious side dish.

1 or 1½ cups leftover mashed potatoes	*medium mixing bowl*
	measuring cup and spoons
1 egg	*fork*
1 tsp powdered sage	*mixing spoon*
1 tsp chopped onion	*skillet*
1 tbsp chopped parsley	*spatula*

Put leftover potatoes into mixing bowl. Break an egg into the measuring cup you used for the potatoes. (No need to wash it first.) Beat the egg with a fork until well mixed and fluffy. Add to mashed potatoes and mix well.

If you like, add sage, or onion, or parsley—or all three.

Heat 2 tablespoons butter or margarine in skillet over medium heat. Drop in spoonfuls of potato mixture. Flatten and spread into patty shape with a fork. Cook about 3 to 5 minutes on each side, until well heated and crispy brown. Use a spatula to turn patties over.

Add butter or margarine, sour cream, or gravy. *Serves 4 to 6.*

Astrofact: The principle known as action and reaction causes a rocket to work. When flames rush out of the tail of a rocket, that's the action. Reaction to the rush of flames makes the rocket move forward.

☆ BOOSTER ROCKETS

These won't really give an extra burst of speed to a spaceship, but they will add a tasty boost to a wintertime supper.

4 yams or sweet potatoes	*vegetable brush*
all about the same size	*cookie sheet*
	aluminum foil

Turn oven on to 350 degrees.

Scrub yams or sweet potatoes well with vegetable brush. Pull off a piece of aluminum foil large enough so all four potatoes can be placed on it. Put foil on cookie sheet and put potatoes on foil. Bake until tender when tested with a fork. (At 350 degrees, medium-sized potatoes will be done in about 45 minutes. But the temperature can be as low as 325 if the potatoes are cooked longer. Or it can be as high as 450, in which case the potatoes will cook much more quickly, perhaps in 25 minutes.)

To save energy, plan to serve Booster Rockets when the oven is being used for something else. For example, if a casserole is being baked at 350 degrees for thirty minutes, start the potatoes 15 minutes before the casserole goes into the oven. Or, if a pie is being baked at 450 degrees for one hour, put the potatoes in after the pie has been baking for 30 minutes. *Serves 4.*

Astrotip: Booster Rockets are delicious with sour cream and chives or with butter or margarine.

Astrofact: The three primary substances of which Earth consists—water, land, and air—are known as hydrosphere, geosphere and atmosphere.

☆ MARS MUDDLE

Creamy Mars-colored mixture to serve over crispy crackers.

1 10½-oz can condensed	*small bowl*
tomato soup	*can opener*
¼ cup milk	*potholders or mitts*
¼ lb Cheddar cheese	*small saucepan*
8 crackers	*grater*
	measuring cup
	mixing spoon
	4 soup bowls

Put soup and milk into saucepan. Grate cheese, slanting grater away from your body, into small bowl. (Keep fingers away from sharp edges.) Add cheese to soup mixture. Cook over low heat, stirring so the cheese melts completely. Keep warm while you place two crackers in each soup bowl. Pour Mars Muddle over crackers and serve. *Serves 4.*

Astrotwister: Say this six times swiftly: Star Glow Triad Squash.

☆☆ STAR GLOW TRIAD

Three shades of squash, highlighted with cheese, make an eye-catching, taste-tempting vegetable dish.

½ cup water
2 small zucchini squash
 (dark green)
2 small crookneck squash
 (yellow)
2 small patty-pan squash
 (pale green)
⅓ cup cheese
 (Monterey Jack or
 Cheddar)

medium saucepan with lid
measuring cups
paring knife
cutting board
spoon
grater
potholders or mitts
serving bowl

Bring ½ cup water to boil in covered saucepan over medium heat. Wash squash but do not peel. Cut off stem and blossom end. With paring knife and cutting board, cut zucchini and crookneck in ½ inch slices. Cut patty-pan in quarters. When water is boiling, carefully lower squash into saucepan. (Younger astrocooks should ask an adult to help.) Adding the squash will cool the boiling water slightly. Replace cover on pan and leave heat at medium until water comes to a boil again. Then turn heat to low and simmer 10 to 15 minutes until squash is just barely tender when tested with a fork. (When testing, use potholders or mitts and lift the lid away from your body so the steam will rise on the opposite side of the pan.) While squash cooks, grate the cheese. When vegetables are tender, drain off any cooking water which remains. (Again, younger astrocooks should ask for help.) Spoon squash into serving bowl and sprinkle with grated cheese. *Serves 3 to 6.*

Astrofact: The invisible force which holds the universe together is known as gravity.

Astrojoke: How can an astrocook on Earth change a tomato
into another vegetable? *Toss it in the air and it comes
down squash.*

☆☆ SUN GRAZER MIX

Comet tails contain glittery ice, frozen gasses and meteoroidal materials. If collected together, they might resemble
this colorful vegetable mix.

1 5-oz can water chestnuts	*strainer*
1 10-oz package frozen	*paring knife*
green peas	*cutting board*
¼ lb fresh mushrooms	*paper towels*
½ cup water	*saucepan with lid*
½ tsp salt	*8-inch skillet*
2 tbsp butter or margarine	*spatula*
pepper	*serving bowl*
	large spoon
	potholder or mitt

Drain water chestnuts in strainer. Place on cutting board
and chop into pieces with paring knife. Pour into serving
bowl and set aside.

Use damp paper towels to clean all outside surfaces of the
mushrooms, then place on the cutting board. With paring
knife cut off stem ends, then cut each mushroom into 3 or 4
slices. Set aside.

Put water and salt into saucepan. Cover pan and bring to a
boil over medium heat. Add frozen peas to the boiling water

in saucepan. Bring to a second boil, then cover the pan and turn the heat to low. Simmer 5 minutes.

While peas cook, melt butter or margarine in skillet over low heat. Add mushroom slices. Stir with spatula for 3 to 4 minutes while slices brown.

Protect hands with potholder or mitt while you drain water from cooked peas. Pour peas into serving bowl with water chestnuts, add browned mushrooms, and sprinkle with pepper. Mix all ingredients gently with large spoon. Serve while hot. *Serves 6.*

Astroriddle: How do you spell astrocook backwards? *a-s-t-r-o-c-o-o-k-b-a-c-k-w-a-r-d-s.*

Astrofact: Like other planets, the dark side of Earth is the side turned away from the sun.

EARTH PUZZLE

Across:

1. An exploding star is called a Super_____.
4. Comets called "sun grazers" make part of their _____ close to the sun.
5. A rocket works on the _____ of action and reaction.
7. Scientists haven't yet discovered why a _____ will sometimes explode.
8. We live in the Milky Way _____.

Down:

2. Some comets pass through the sun's outer _____.
3. The dark side is the part of a _____ which has turned away from its sun.
6. Earth's _____ substances are water, land, and air.

MARS MEDLIES
Salads

The Moon Cheese War

Inigo was palace kitchen cleaner on the planet of Ethban from the time he was old enough to hold a broom. When he was old enough to hold a spoon, Inigo became cook's apprentice. From there he went on to create wonderful recipes.

The king often sent a pearl or a ruby to the kitchen to show his thanks for Inigo's talent. Unfortunately, such praise went to Inigo's head. He saw that the king often sent small bags of gold to thank the old cook for special dinners.

"Why shouldn't I get bags of gold and the jewels as well?" Inigo asked himself. "I'm better than the old cook ever was."

Inigo thought of a plan. When the old cook asked for pepper, Inigo the apprentice filled the pepper jar with sand. When the old cook asked for a cup of sugar, Inigo the apprentice gave him a cup of salt instead. The king was so upset, he sent the old cook to live on a wheel colony between the planet Ethban and its moon.

Then the king made apprentice Inigo chief cook of the palace kitchen. A young girl named Denia was brought in as Inigo's new apprentice.

Inigo was pleased. "The old cook *was* too old," he told himself, and set about making wonderful dishes to please the king.

As time went on, Denia thought of new and wonderful dishes of her own. Inigo always sent Denia's dishes to the king. But he never told the king they were Denia's ideas.

"Denia is young," Inigo said to himself. "Praise too early would spoil her." Then he slipped the king's gift of a ruby or pearl into his pocket and told Denia to get on with her work.

One day a member of the court came into the kitchen with a pearl from the king and said that the salmon cake had pleased the king greatly. Denia smiled. But Inigo frowned and told her to get busy shaping moon cheese into balls to serve with the queen's crackers and tea.

He put the pearl into his pocket and went on arranging a raspberry gelatin ring for the king's dessert. He could see that Denia was angry because the salmon cake was her idea. "It's time to get a new apprentice," Inigo told himself. "Denia is beginning to get too many ideas."

Suddenly, a moon cheese ball whizzed by Inigo's face and stuck on the wall behind him. He looked up, startled. There was Denia, balancing a second moon cheese ball on the tip of a long metal spatula.

"You lied," she shouted. She pulled the spatula back and hurled the ball at Inigo. It landed right in the gelatin ring.

"You're fired!" Inigo shouted.

"Only the king can fire who the king hires," Denia said. Then she hurled more moon cheese balls at Inigo.

Some hit the wall; some hit his face; many stuck in the raspberry gelatin.

Inigo grabbed the dessert and rushed into the king's dining room. "Your Majesty," he cried, "just see what that apprentice has done to your dessert."

"Hmmm," the king said, "moon cheese balls in raspberry gelatin. What an idea." He took a bite. Then he took another bite. Then he smiled.

He looked up at Inigo. "Go wash your face," the king said, "you're a mess." Then he added, "This moon cheese gelatin is the best idea that ever came from my kitchen. I hereby name Denia chief palace cook."

☆☆ MOON CHEESE SALAD BALLS

Here is Denia's recipe for you. The cheese balls should be no larger than peas. Double the recipe and use a 1-quart mold for a party.

1 3-oz package wild raspberry gelatin	*measuring cup*
	large bowl
1 3-oz package cream cheese	*mixing spoon*
	saucer
½ cup walnuts, ground	*nut grinder or knife and cutting board*
1 10-oz package raspberries, frozen in syrup	*2-cup ring mold for gelatin*
1¼ cups water	*small saucepan with lid*
lettuce or parsley	*serving plate*

Follow thawing instructions on raspberry package. While berries thaw, pour gelatin into bowl. Pour 1¼ cups water into saucepan, cover, and bring to a boil. Younger astrocooks should ask an adult to help measure 1 cup of boiling water into gelatin. Stir until gelatin dissolves.

Put walnuts through nut grinder or chop them very fine

with the knife and cutting board. Place in saucer. With very clean hands and fingernails, break small chunks of cream cheese from the package. Roll lightly with your fingers to form balls the size of peas. Roll each cheese ball in crushed walnuts until well covered. Repeat until all the cream cheese is used.

Put thawed berries into the cooled gelatin and pour into ring mold. Gelatin will begin to thicken. Poke the walnut-covered balls into the gelatin all the way around the ring. Refrigerate until ready to serve. Then dip the bottom of the ring mold briefly in warm water. Don't let the water come over the top of the mold into the gelatin. Place serving plate over the ring and quickly turn the plate and mold upside down, so the plate is on the bottom. Lift off the mold. Poke lettuce or parsley around the gelatin edges and serve. *Serves 3 to 4.*

Astrofact: Mars, the red planet, has two satellites. A year on Mars is almost twice as long as a year on Earth, since Mars is farther from the sun and takes longer (687 days) to orbit that big star. Viking I and II were launched by the United States to land on Mars and send back photos and information. Mars is brilliant orange-red and rocky. It has the largest known volcano in the solar system (over 300 miles wide at the base) and three other volcanoes each over 200 miles wide.

Astrojoke:
Astroguest: "What's brown and furry and has six legs?"
Astrocook: "I don't know."
Astroguest: "You'd better find out. It's crawling on the salad."

☆☆ LUNAR CHEESE SALAD

In the past some people said the moon was made of green cheese.

1 3-oz package lime
  gelatin
1¼ cups water
1 cup chilled pineapple
  juice
1 8-oz can crushed
  pineapple, undrained
1 cup sour cream
1 cup cottage cheese

small saucepan with lid
mixing bowl
mixing spoon
measuring cup
square cake pan or
  dessert dishes

Early in the morning or the day before, place can of pineapple juice in the refrigerator to chill. When ready to make salad, bring 1¼ cups water to boil in small saucepan. (To save energy, use a covered saucepan—the water will boil more quickly.) Empty contents of gelatin box into mixing bowl. Ask an adult to help measure one cup boiling water and pour it into the gelatin. Stir until gelatin dissolves.

Add pineapple juice, sour cream, and cottage cheese to gelatin. Mix until well blended, then stir in crushed pineapple. Pour into square cake pan or individual dessert dishes. (If using cake pan, cut salad into squares or diamonds to serve. Lift out of pan with spatula or pancake turner.) This salad is especially attractive when served on a leaf of red lettuce and garnished with a few sprigs of green parsley. *Serves 4 to 6.*

Astroriddle: If you don't want to offend a Martian astrocook, should you eat your salad with your right hand or your left hand? *You should eat your salad with a fork.*

Avocado rings and sliced eggs make a colorful solar salad in a
green lettuce sky.

2 avocados	*saucepan*
2 eggs	*paring knife*
¼ cup corn chips	*cutting board*
lettuce	*paper towels*
	salad bowl
	rolling pin
	plastic bag or waxed paper

Hard-cook eggs by putting them in a saucepan and adding
cold water to cover. Place on medium heat until water just
begins to boil. Turn off heat. Leave eggs in water for 25
minutes.

Rinse lettuce under cold water. Pat dry with paper towels. Place leaves in salad bowl to cover bottom. Peel avocados and slice into rings by running paring knife through
the fruit to the pit. Turn the avocado so the knife slices all
the way around in a ring. Slide rings off pit and place on
lettuce in bowl.

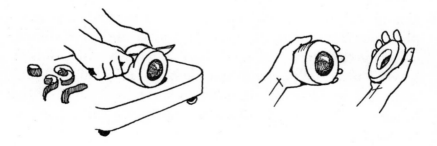

Remove shells from hard-cooked eggs. Use paring knife to
cut eggs into round slices. Handle carefully so the yolk
doesn't fall out. Place egg slices in bowl with avocado rings.

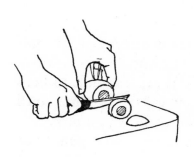

Put the corn chips in a plastic bag or in a fold of waxed paper. Run the rolling pin over the bag several times to crush the chips. Sprinkle crushed chips over the salad. Serve with Mars Moon Dressing from this chapter, or with your own favorite dressing. *Serves 3 to 4.*

Astroextra: Save avocado pits to start a plant. Just poke the seed halfway into a pot of earth, point end up, and keep watered.

Astrotwister: Say this fast several times. Shawn shuttles salads.

☆☆ UNIVERSE SALAD

T   salad is a universal favorite for potatoes.

4 medium potatoes	*2 saucepans with lids*
4 eggs	*potholders or mitts*
½ cup chopped onion	*paring knife*
1 large pickle (dill	*cutting board*
or sweet)	*large mixing bowl*
2 small or 1 large	*measuring cup*
celery stick	*tablespoon*
mayonnaise or salad	*mixing spoon*
dressing	
paprika	
salt and pepper	

Put four cups of water into medium-size saucepan, put on lid, place over medium heat and bring to a boil. Wash potatoes. (Younger astrocooks should ask an adult to help lower the potatoes into the boiling water.) Simmer until potatoes feel tender when you poke them with a fork.

While potatoes cook, place eggs in small saucepan. Pour in just enough cold water to cover the eggs, place over medium heat, cover pan, and bring to a boil. Turn off heat and leave eggs in covered pan for 25 minutes. Pour off the water and allow eggs to cool, but do not chill. When potatoes are tender, ask an adult to help pour off the water. Set the potatoes aside until cool enough to handle.

While potatoes and eggs are cooling, chop onion, pickle, and celery. (Use the cutting board and always slant the knife away from your fingers.)

Peel potatoes, chop into small chunks, and place in large mixing bowl. Peel eggs, chop, and add to the potatoes. Sprinkle lightly with salt and pepper. Add onions, pickles, and celery and mix well. Add 4 tablespoons mayonnaise. Stir well. Add more mayonnaise, one tablespoon at a time, until mixture is well moistened. Sprinkle lightly with paprika. Chill salad until ready to serve. *Serves 4 to 6.*

Astroriddle: When is a galactic guest most likely to enter the astrocook's kitchen? *When the door is open.*

Astrofact: Both Earth and Mars have polar caps, but on Earth they're made of frozen water, while on Mars they're made of frozen carbon dioxide (dry ice).

Astroriddle: How many balls of string would you need to reach from a garden on Earth to a bubble colony on the Moon? *One—if it was long enough.*

☆☆ SPACE SHUTTLES

Fill avocado halves with shrimp and shuttle to the table.

1 ripe avocado
1 4½-oz can cooked
  salad shrimp
1 tomato, medium size
1 4½-oz can black
  olive slices
1 green onion with stem
lettuce
¼ tsp salt
dash pepper
2 tbsp French salad
  dressing
½ tbsp vinegar
½ tbsp water

paring knife
cutting board
strainer
small bowl
medium bowl
2 salad plates
measuring spoons
paper towels

In small bowl mix together sauce ingredients—French dressing, vinegar, water, salt, and pepper.

Pour shrimp into strainer, rinse under cold running water, and put into medium-size bowl. Drain olive slices in strainer. Use knife and cutting board to chop tomato into small pieces. Slice green onion into thin rounds. Add olives, tomato, and onion to shrimp.

Wash two large lettuce leaves, pat dry with paper towels, and place on individual salad plates. Slice avocado in half lengthwise, cutting through fruit to the pit, all the way around. Pull halves apart and put each on a lettuce leaf in salad plate.

Pour sauce over shrimp and vegetables. Mix gently. Spoon onto avocados. Refrigerate until ready to serve. *Serves 2.*

Create your own Martians or space aliens by putting together fresh raw vegetables. Serve Deimos or Mars Moon Dressing in bowls as dips for dunking vegetable bits.

Suggested fresh vegetables:

cherry tomatoes	*paring knife*
radishes	*cutting board*
mushroom caps	*paper towels*
cucumber, cut in slices	*vegetable tray*
or chunks	*salad plates*
carrot sticks	
celery sticks	

Clean mushroom caps by wiping with damp paper towel. Wash remaining vegetables in cold water. Pat with paper towels to dry. Arrange vegetables on tray.

Have each person try to make the funniest space creature by putting vegetable pieces together on a salad plate. Cherry tomatoes or radishes might be used for heads, cucumber chunks for bodies, carrot sticks or celery sticks for arms and legs. Celery sticks can be cut into a fringe for a skirt. Mushrooms can be used for caps. You will think of other ways to arrange your vegetable creatures.

Astrotwister: Say this five times fast: Cottage cheese swirls.

☆☆ LASER MIX

This salad adds a touch of laser-bright color to your table.

⅓ cup raisins
1 cup water
about 6 medium carrots
¼ cup crushed pineapple
mayonnaise or salad
    dressing

saucepan with lid
small bowl
salad bowl
vegetable brush
mixing spoon
grater
plastic wrap
strainer

Put one cup water into small saucepan, cover, and place over medium heat and bring to a boil. Turn off heat. Put the raisins in a small bowl. Younger astrocooks should ask an adult to help pour enough boiling water over the raisins to cover them. Set aside.

Drain ¼ cup pineapple in strainer. (Save juice, add to any fruit drink.)

Scrub carrots. Grate them into a salad bowl. (To grate, always begin with the narrow end of the carrot. Keep your fingers away from the sharp edges of the grater. Don't try to use the last inch of carrot.)

Add pineapple to carrots in bowl. Drain water from raisins and add them to the carrot/pineapple mixture. Stir well. Add two or three tablespoons of mayonnaise or salad dressing and stir together. If necessary add more mayonnaise or dressing, one tablespoon at a time, until salad is well moistened. Cover with plastic wrap. Chill until ready to serve. *Serves 4.*

Astroextra: For a different flavor, add any or all of the following ingredients to your Laser Mix salad:

¼ cup chopped green pepper
¼ cup chopped onion
¼ cup chopped nuts
½ cup grated apple
¼ cup chopped celery
½ cup grated zucchini

or: Use only 3 carrots and add 1 cup chopped or grated cabbage.

Astrofact: Natural satellites are small planets revolving around larger ones. Earth has one satellite, known as the moon. Mars and Neptune each have two. Uranus has five. Saturn has ten. Jupiter has thirteen. If Mercury, Venus, and Pluto have satellites, they have not yet been discovered.

☆ MARS SALAD I

Red salad—the perfect salad to serve on the red planet, Mars.

red or ruby leaf lettuce	*paring knife*
choice of dressings	*cutting board*
	paper towels
	salad bowl

Cut tough stem end from head of lettuce, separate leaves, wash gently under cold running water, shake, spread on paper towels and pat dry. Tear lettuce into small pieces. Use enough leaves to fill a large salad bowl or individual bowls, one for each member of the crew.

Pass dressing in a bowl so crew members can add as much as they like. See Phobos and Deimos Dressing below.

☆ MARS MOON DRESSINGS

Mars was named for a god of war in Greek mythology. The planet's two natural satellites (or moons) were named Phobos (fear) and Deimos (terror) after sons of the mythological god.

☆ PHOBOS DRESSING

3 tbsp mayonnaise *measuring spoons*
2 tbsp ketchup *small bowl*
1 or 2 tsp pickle juice, *fork*
 sweet or dill
pinch of thyme or basil

Place mayonnaise, ketchup, and pickle juice in bowl. If you like, add a pinch of dried thyme or basil. Stir with fork until well blended. Cover and chill in refrigerator until ready to serve.

☆ DEIMOS DRESSING

2 tbsp mayonnaise *measuring spoons*
2 tbsp sour cream *small bowl*
2 tbsp buttermilk *fork*
pinch of garlic powder

Place mayonnaise, sour cream, and buttermilk in bowl. Add a pinch of garlic powder and stir with fork until well blended. Cover and chill until ready to serve.

Astroextra: To make an Earth Green Salad, prepare green lettuce as directed in Mars Salad I. Add your choice of—or all—the following ingredients to the lettuce in the salad bowl:

> chopped celery
> chopped celery leaves
> chopped onion
> chopped green onions
> chopped parsley
> sliced tomatoes
> whole cherry tomatoes
> chopped green pepper
> sliced radishes
> grated carrots
> grated zucchini squash
> sliced hard-cooked eggs
> croutons
> leftover cooked vegetables, chilled
> cold chopped chicken, turkey, or ham

Serve with your favorite Mars Moon Dressing or offer a choice of dressings.

Astroriddle: What did the space commander say to the salad cook? *Don't come to the table without dressing.*

☆ MARS SALAD II

(Another red one.)

4 whole tomatoes	*paring knife*
2 hard-cooked eggs	*cutting board*
mayonnaise	*salad bowl*
1 tsp chopped parsley	*mixing spoon*
paprika	*saucepan with lid*
salt	*salad plates*
pepper	

To hard-cook eggs, place in saucepan, add just enough cold water to cover the eggs, place lid on pan, turn heat to medium, and cook just until the water begins to boil. Turn off heat and leave pan covered for 25 minutes. Pour off water and chill eggs until ready to use.

When ready to make salad, peel the eggs, place in a bowl, and mash them with a fork. Add just enough mayonnaise, one tablespoon at a time, to blend the egg together well. Add chopped parsley and sprinkle lightly with salt and pepper.

Make three cuts down through the tomato, spaced evenly apart, but don't cut all the way through the bottom. Gently spread the tomato apart. It will open like six petals of a flower.

Use a spoon to fill each opened tomato with an equal share of the egg mixture. Sprinkle lightly with paprika. Serve on lettuce leaves on individual salad plates. *Serves 4.*

For the third red salad, prepare tomatoes as directed above, but add the following tuna mixture.

celery	*paring knife*
sweet pickle or relish	*cutting board*
1 can tuna	*bowl*
mayonnaise	*mixing spoon*
	measuring spoons

Chop enough celery and sweet pickles to measure two tablespoons *each*. Drain the oil from a can of tuna and scrape the fish into a bowl. Add celery, sweet pickle or relish, and stir. Now add enough mayonnaise to moisten and blend well. *Serves 4.*

Astroextra: This tuna mix is also good as a spread for sandwiches or crackers. For another salad variation, try tomatoes stuffed with cottage cheese or the Unidentified Flyer mix in Chapter 8.

Astrotip: For a simple salad, place ⅓ cup cottage cheese on a lettuce leaf and add tomato or slices of fresh or canned fruits.

Astroriddle: Which Martian astrocook wears the largest hat? *The one with the largest head.*

Astrofact: An immense canyon—3½ miles deep at many points—stretches along the equator of the planet Mars. If placed on Earth, the canyon would run from Boston to San Francisco. (The Grand Canyon would be no more than a scratch in comparison.) Yet Mars is only half the size of Earth.

MARS PUZZLE

Across:
3. What color is Mars? (two words)
6. Mars has the largest known _____ in the solar system.
7. What does Mars orbit?
9. Name of Mars' closest moon.

Down:
1. Name of natives once believed to live on Mars.
2. Name of Mars' outer moon.
4. Mars has two _____.
5. If on Earth, this Martian feature would reach from San Francisco to Boston.
6. Name of the mission that first landed on Mars.
8. Mars is the _____ planet from the sun.

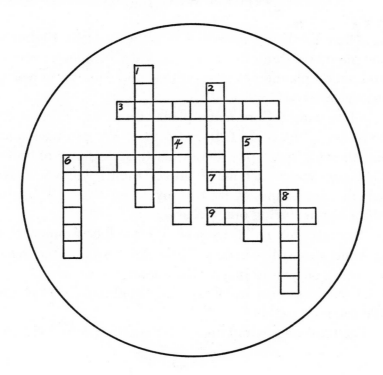

JUPITER JUMBLES
Breads

Who's Laughing?

When Earth was accepted into the Galactic Federation, the planet celebrated with a Solar Fair. People of every race and nation planned games, parties, and contests to welcome intergalactic visitors.

A boy named Gary made plans of his own. "This is going to be wild," he told his friend Anne. "We can have a lot of fun showing space people our Earth-style sense of humor."

"Gary, you won't make fun of them, will you?" Anne asked. "Sometimes it isn't funny when you yell insults at other teams during our soccer games."

"Sure, it's funny," Gary said. "This will be funniest of all."

Anne was still worried. "Just don't forget, the team is counting on you to play in the soccer tournament."

"I wouldn't miss it," Gary said, laughing. "Where would the team be without me?"

The tournament and many Fair contests were held on the

same days, but there was plenty of time between games for Gary to poke fun at the weird extraterrestrials.

"Get a horse!" he yelled at the flying Pluton whose wings were too small to lift him in Earth's heavier gravity.

"Welcome to Earth," he said to a Jovian, shaking its elephantine snout instead of its arm-tendril until the creature sneezed so hard it almost blew itself off the ground.

The contests were the most fun. Gary went from one to another joking with the visitors, until he came to the Braxtl-Bread Eating Contest. He decided to enter. When he took his first bite of the loaf-shaped Braxtl Bread, he understood why most contestants were natives. The bread tasted like clay mixed with sand.

When Gary saw the tiny little bites the Braxtlians took, slurping the bread through their tubular mouths, he could hardly eat for laughing.

"This is what you look like," he said to the Braxtl next to him and twisted his mouth to eat.

"This is what you sound like," he said to the Braxtl on his other side, and slurped the bread until he almost choked from laughing. He was having too much fun to mind the awful taste.

When the contest was over, Gary had eaten the most bread in the shortest time. "First prize is an instant trip to Braxtl," cried the announcer.

Before Gary could say, "but I've got a game in ten minutes," he was pushed into a teleport cage. The next thing he knew he was standing on a lighted disk in a grove of Braxtl trees. The claylike loaves that were the natives' only food hung heavy from branches. Pickers stared, then bent over snorting with laughter.

A Braxtlian squatting near Gary looked at him in surprise. "Why are they using the teleport cage so soon?" he demanded. "They know it will be two or three Earth weeks before I get the return trip working."

Before Gary could answer, the Braxtlian bent over snorting with laughter. "Sorry," it gasped. "You'll be our guest, of course. But I can't help laughing. You look so funny!"

Astrofact: The largest planet, Jupiter, is 88,700 miles in diameter and 483 million miles away from the sun. Jupiter has 13 satellites. A year on Jupiter is as long as 12 years on Earth. This planet rotates faster than Earth does, so a day and night together on Jupiter is not quite 10 hours. Jupiter is the doorway to the outer planets—and to the void of interstellar space.

☆☆ SHUTTLE MUFFINS

If Gary had taken this refrigerator mix along, he could have had a good-tasting bread to eat on Braxtl while waiting to return to earth.

1⅓ cups water	*small saucepan*
1 cup 100% bran *or* bran buds	*potholders or mitts*
½ cup vegetable shortening	*measuring cups and spoons*
1½ cups sugar	*large and medium mixing bowls*
2 eggs	*mixing spoon*
2 cups buttermilk	*electric mixer*
2½ cups flour	*flour sifter*
2½ tsp baking soda	*large covered refrigerator-container or*
½ tsp salt	*muffin tins*
2 cups All Bran cereal	
1 cup raisins	

Place 1⅓ cups water into saucepan, cover, and bring to a boil. While water heats, measure shortening.

84

Astrotip: To measure solid vegetable shortening, fill a measuring cup with water to the ½-cup line. Spoon in shortening until water level rises to the 1-cup line. You now have ½-cup shortening and ½-cup water. Carefully pour off the water. Place shortening into large mixing bowl and set aside.

Place 1 cup bran or bran buds in medium bowl. Measure out 1 cup of boiling water (younger astrocooks should ask an adult to help) and pour over the bran. Stir and set aside.

Place mixing bowl with shortening under blades of electric mixer. (If you haven't used the mixer before, ask an adult for directions or mix the batter by hand.) Whip shortening until creamy and turn off mixer.

Sprinkle ½ cup sugar over the shortening and mix well. Repeat two times until all the sugar has been added and the mixture is light and creamy.

Add eggs, one at a time, beating well after each addition. Remove bowl to work surface. Rinse mixer blades or soak in soapy water.

Add buttermilk and bran mixture to the sugar, shortening, and egg mix. Blend with mixing spoon. Sift flour with soda and salt and add to mixture. Add All Bran cereal and raisins. Stir until all dry ingredients are thoroughly moistened. Batter is now ready to bake or to store in covered container in refrigerator and shuttle to the oven when needed. (Mixture will keep for six weeks.)

To bake, heat oven to 400 degrees. Grease muffin cups and fill each one ⅔ full with muffin batter. Bake 25 minutes. *Makes 2½ dozen muffins.*

Astrofact: Some scientists believe Jupiter may be a star, rather than a planet. Like a star, Jupiter consists of gasses such as ammonia and hydrogen sulfide. Also, it radiates twice the energy it receives from our sun. (Normally energy is produced by a star or sun and absorbed by planets.)

Astroknock Knock: Who's there? Samoa. Samoa who? Samoa that Battlestar Bread would sure taste good right now.

☆☆☆ BATTLESTAR BREAD

It's called a bread, but it tastes like a cake—whatever name you give it, it's delicious.

1 cup water	*small saucepan*
2 eggs	*2 small bowls*
butter or margarine	*8-inch ovenproof baking*
¾ cup raisins	*bowl*
2 to 4 zucchini squash,	*small and large mixing*
depending on size	*bowls*
¾ cup vegetable oil	*grater*
½ cup honey	*eggbeater*
¾ tsp vanilla	*measuring cups and spoons*
1½ cups whole wheat flour	*mixing spoon*
¾ cup unbleached flour	*narrow spatula*
2 tsp baking powder	*serving plate*
1½ tsp cinnamon	*potholders or mitts*
¼ tsp cloves	*hot pad*
½ tsp salt	*serving dish*
¾ cup chopped nuts and/or	*waxed paper*
sunflower seeds	
1 dozen whole almonds,	
optional	
confectioners' sugar, optional	

Remove eggs from refrigerator. Place in small bowl (so they won't roll) and leave on counter to warm to room temperature.

86

Put water in small saucepan, cover, and bring to a boil. Place raisins in second small bowl. Pour in just enough boiling water to cover the raisins. (Younger astrocooks should ask an adult to pour boiling water.) Set raisins aside.

With a small fold of waxed paper, spread a thick layer of butter or margarine all over the inside of an ovenproof baking bowl. This will keep the bread from sticking. Set bowl aside.

Wash zucchini, but do not peel. Slant grater away from you into small mixing bowl. Keep your fingers away from sharp edges as you push zucchini against the grater blades. Grate enough to make 2¼ cups and set aside.

Turn oven on to 350 degrees.

Break eggs into large mixing bowl and whip with eggbeater until light and frothy. Add oil, honey, and vanilla and stir gently. Add flour, baking powder, spices, and salt. Mix gently until all ingredients are well blended.

Drain water from raisins. Pour off any liquid that may have drained out of the grated zucchini. Add nuts, raisins, and zucchini to bread batter and mix well.

Pour batter into greased ovenproof bowl and bake at 350 degrees for about one hour, or until firm and lightly browned.

Place hot pad on kitchen counter or table. Using mitts or potholders, carefully remove baking bowl from oven and place on hot pad. Allow to cool about ten minutes before removing bread from bowl. Then, carefully slide a narrow spatula between bread and the sides of the bowl to loosen

the edges. Place serving dish upside down over the bowl.

With one hand on each side, holding both bowl and serving dish, flip them so the bowl is resting upside down on the plate. (It's easier than it sounds. If you've never tried it before, practice with an empty plastic bowl and plate.)

Let bowl stand upside down on serving dish until bread drops. If necessary tap the bowl a few times to help loosen the bread.

For an everyday dessert, serve Battlestar Bread warm or cold, with or without butter, margarine, peanut butter or honey.

For a party dessert, sprinkle with confectioners' sugar while bread is still warm. Stud with almonds, poking them into the bread at equal intervals, all the way around, about one inch from the bottom, like this:
Serves 8 or more.

Astroextra: See Chapter 11 for tips on fortunetelling with Battlestar Bread.

Astroknock Knock: Who's there? Jupiter. Jupiter who? Can't find the cat. Jupiter out?

Astrojoke:
> First Space Colonist: Why don't you start a bakery on Jupiter?
>
> Second Space Colonist: I will, as soon as I raise enough dough!

☆☆ LANDING PADS

Do-it-yourself crackers for better flavor, better nutrition.

1 cup whole wheat flour	*large mixing bowl*
1 cup unbleached flour	*measuring cups and spoons*
¼ cup wheat germ	*2 table knives or pastry*
extra flour for rolling	*blender*
pin and towel	*clean dish towel*
1½ tsp caraway *or*	*rolling pin*
dill seeds	*drinking glass*
1 tsp salt	*spatula*
½ tsp baking soda	*cookie sheet*
1 cup peanut butter	
½ cup water	
2 tbsp cider vinegar	

Place whole wheat flour, unbleached flour, wheat germ, caraway or dill seeds, salt, baking soda, and peanut butter into large mixing bowl. Cut peanut butter into the other ingredients with pastry blender or two knives. (With knives, take one in each hand, crisscross them so each blade touches the other and your hands are close together. As you pull your hands away from each other, pull the blade of one knife close to the blade of the other knife, with a small amount of peanut butter between. Repeat over and over until peanut butter has been cut into tiny pieces and well blended with dry ingredients.)

Add water and vinegar and mix until dough holds to-gether. If dough is too dry, add a bit more water, one table-spoon at a time. You want the dough to hold its shape when you form it into a ball, but you don't want it sticky.

Turn oven on to 375 degrees. Divide ball of dough in half. Spread a clean dry dish towel out on your work surface. Lightly dust the towel and rolling pin with flour. Roll half of dough out until it is about ⅛ inch thick. Cut into circles with the top of a drinking glass. Set the scraps aside.

Using a spatula, carefully lift each circle of dough and place about ½ inch apart on an ungreased cookie sheet. Repeat with second half of dough. Pat the scraps into a ball, roll out, and cut them into squares.

Bake Landing Pads at 375 degrees for 10 to 15 minutes, or until lightly browned and crispy. Watch carefully after the first 10 minutes so they don't get too brown.

Makes about 40 crackers, delicious just as they come from the oven and even better when used as landing pads for cream cheese, peanut butter, honey, or your favorite sandwich spread. If your crew doesn't finish them all in one sitting, store extras in an airtight container.

Astrofact: The planet Jupiter has thirteen moons. Or— Jupiter could be a star with thirteen planets.

Astroriddle: Why are eggs on planet Pegasus like the ones in a space colony? *They must be broken before they can be used.*

Astrofact: Scientists have already begun making plans for colonies to be built in space. They may be shaped like cylinders, spheres, wheels, or hatboxes. Some colonies may provide living quarters, farming lands, and manufac-turing plants for 2,000, 10,000 or even as many as 140,000 people.

☆☆☆ COLONY LOAF

This tangy bread is filled with green olive slices that look like wheel (or Torus) colonies.

1 cup pimento-stuffed
   olives
¼ lb Cheddar cheese
1 egg
1½ cups buttermilk
3 cups biscuit mix
2 tbsp sugar

measuring cups and spoons
large mixing bowl
mixing spoon
9×5×3 inch loaf pan
cooling rack
plastic wrap

Cut each green olive into three slices and set aside. Grate cheese, slanting grater away from you into bowl. Keep fingers from sharp edges as you grate, then set aside. Turn oven on to 350 degrees. Beat egg in large mixing bowl. Add buttermilk, biscuit mix, and sugar and beat together until well blended. Stir in grated cheese and sliced green olives.

Grease the sides and bottom of the loaf pan with butter or margarine, then carefully pour in the bread batter. Bake at 350 degrees for 50 minutes. Use potholders or mitts to remove pan to cooling rack. Cool for five minutes before turning loaf out of pan onto rack. Leave loaf on rack until well cooled. To serve, cut slices with thin sharp knife. Good as is or spread with butter, margarine, or cream cheese.

Wrap extra bread with plastic wrap and store in refrigerator. *Makes 1 loaf.*

Astrofact: Materials mined from the moon and from asteroids may be used in the space colonies for soil, building materials, and manufacturing.

Astroriddle: When are space colony farmers cruel to their corn? *When they pull its ears.*

☆ SPACE COLONY BISCUITS

Surprise your crew with these specially shaped biscuits for dinner, or serve for lunch with salad and soup, or for breakfast with eggs or Zoom Soup.

⅓ cup butter or margarine
1 package prepared
  biscuits
1 tsp garlic powder
Parmesan cheese

oblong cake pan
measuring cups and spoons
fork
potholders or mitts
hot pad
cutting board
knife

Turn oven on to 350 degrees. Place butter or margarine in cake pan and leave in oven a minute or two, just until butter or margarine is melted. Meanwhile, open the package of prepared biscuits. Place hot pad on work surface.

With potholders or mitts carefully remove pan of melted butter from the oven. (Hot butter burns! Younger astrocooks should ask an adult to help.) Place pan on hot pad. Turn oven to 450.

Using the cutting board, cut each biscuit in half. Roll each piece of dough between the palms of your hands until it is long and thin. Dip strip of dough into melted butter and shape into any kind of space colony you can imagine. If you like, snip off bits of dough and stick onto the colony for disks, mirrors, docking ports, and so on. Your colony might be a wheel shape, cylinder, sphere, coil—what else can you think of. Place colonies at least one inch apart in the pan and sprinkle lightly with Parmesan cheese and garlic powder.

Bake at 450 degrees for about 8 minutes, or until lightly browned. Serve warm with butter, margarine, or cream cheese. *Makes 10-15 biscuits.*

☆ STAR MELTS

Fold golden cheese centers into biscuit bits for a bread that will melt in your mouth faster than a snowball on Jupiter.

1 package refrigerated biscuits	*cutting board*
	knife
3 oz Cheddar cheese	*bread board*
flour	*rolling pin*
3 tbsp butter or margarine	*baking pan*
	hot pad
	potholders or mitts

Sprinkle flour on cutting board. Put one biscuit at a time on the board and flour lightly. Dust rolling pin with flour and roll biscuit until flat. Cut each biscuit into quarters, then set biscuits aside. Turn oven to 350 degrees.

Cut cheese into forty small cubes, then set aside.

Place butter in baking pan and put in oven just long enough to melt the butter. Place hot pad on work surface. Using potholders or mitts, carefully take pan of melted butter from oven and place on hot pad. (Younger astrocooks should ask an adult to help.) Turn oven to 450 degrees.

Wrap each biscuit quarter around a cheese cube. Press edges tightly to seal. Place in pan and roll all sides in the melted butter. Leave in pan. When all biscuit quarters have been wrapped in cheese and rolled in butter, place the pan in 450 degree oven. Bake about 8 minutes or until biscuits are light brown. Especially good served warm, but good cold, too. *Makes 40 small biscuits.*

Astrofact: Pioneer 10 and Pioneer 11 traveled for 20 months to reach Jupiter in 1973, sending back photos and other information.

Astroriddle: The star fleet's coming to dinner. How can you make one six-ounce Venusian shrimp go as far as a hundred pounds of giant Jupiter sea creatures? *Freeze them both and ship them to Earth.*

Astroriddle: What planet was the largest in our solar system before Jupiter was known to be there? *Jupiter.*

Astrofact: The Great Red Spot of Jupiter has been seen from Earth for three centuries. A raging storm deflecting other clouds from the area, it is 50,000 kilometers wide and could hold three Earths, side by side.

☆ RENDEZVOUS RING

Friends will be eager to rendezvous with you when you serve this easy treat.

4 tbsp butter or margarine
1 package refrigerated
  biscuits
⅓ cup chopped nuts and/or
  sunflower seeds
2 tablespoons honey
cinnamon

8-inch round cake pan
measuring cup and spoons
potholders or mitts
hot pad
serving dish

Turn oven on to 350 degrees. Place butter or margarine in cake pan and leave in oven just until butter is melted. Meanwhile, open the package of refrigerated biscuits. Place hot pad on work surface.

With potholders or mitts, carefully remove pan of melted butter from oven. (Younger astrocooks should ask an adult to help.) Place pan on hot pad. Turn oven to 450 degrees.

Separate biscuits and dip each one into the butter, then turn biscuit over and leave it in the pan. Lap the second biscuit half-way over the first one, and continue lapping the biscuits so they form a ring that looks like this:

Bake at 450 degrees for about 8 minutes or until lightly browned. Using potholders or mitts, remove from oven and place on hot pad. Still using potholders or mitts, place serving dish upside down on top of hot baking dish. With one hand on each side, hold pan and dish together and flip so pan is upside down on dish. Biscuits will drop onto plate, still in ring shape. (It's easier than you might think. While

95

biscuits bake, you can practice the flip with an empty cake pan and a plastic plate.)

Drizzle warm biscuits with honey and sprinkle with nuts and/or sunflower seeds. Dust lightly with cinnamon and serve at once. *Serves 4.*

Astrotip: Rendezvous Ring is good for breakfast with cottage cheese and fruit, scrambled eggs, or Zoom Soup. Also good for dessert, served warm or cold.

☆☆☆ FAR-OUT SANDWICH SAUCERS

Far-out is what you'll say when you taste one of these saucers stuffed with your favorite sandwich mix.

butter or margarine	*cookie sheets*
2½ cups warm water	*large mixing bowl*
(about 110 degrees)	*mixing spoon*
2 envelopes active dry	*measuring cups and spoons*
yeast	*rolling pin*
1 tsp honey	*potholders or mitts*
1½ tbsp salt	*knife*
1 tbsp vegetable oil	*pancake turner*
6 cups flour	*4 clean dish towels*
extra flour for dusting	
towels and rolling pin	
4 clean dish towels	

Pour warm water into large mixing bowl. (The water should be quite warm, but not too hot to touch, or the yeast won't work properly.) Sprinkle dry yeast over water and stir gently until all grains are dissolved. Stir in honey, salt, and oil.

Stir in five cups of flour, one at a time. Mix well after each addition. Add just enough of the sixth cup of flour to make a sticky dough.

Spread one clean towel on your work surface and dust the towel well with flour so the bread dough won't stick to it. Scrape the dough out of the bowl onto the floured towel. Dust the palms of your hands and your fingers with flour. (Hold your hands over the work counter so you won't be flouring the floor also.) Now knead the dough about ten minutes, until it feels smooth and springy.

(To do this, pat the dough into a firm ball. Push down hard in the middle of the ball with the heels of both hands. Now pull the sides of the ball into the hollow you just made and push again. It's fun to feel the rhythm as you push in the middle and pull the edges back up. Push in the middle and pull the edges back up over and over again.

If your hands get too sticky, stop now and then to rub off any dough which has stuck to them and flour your hands again.)

Now shape the dough into a roll about twelve inches long and place it along the back edge of your cloth. Slice the dough into twelve pieces, each about one inch thick.

If sticky bits of dough remain on your cloth, roll them with the palm of your hand until you can pick off the bits and throw them away. If any dough still sticks to your hands, rub both hands together until the dough rolls off. (Cleanup will be easier if you hold your hands over a trash container while doing this.)

Now wash your hands, dry them well, and dust your hands and cloth once more with flour. Spread a second cloth nearby and dust it with flour also. Spread more flour all over a rolling pin, while holding it over one of the floured cloths.

On the first cloth, roll out one round of dough at a time until it is about ⅛ inch thick. Place each of these bread saucers on the second floured cloth. You may need to dust more flour on the rolling pin from time to time. When all twelve saucers have been rolled out, cover them with a clean dish towel and let stand for two hours. After one hour and 45 minutes, turn oven on to 450 degrees.

Using ungreased cookie sheets, place three saucers on a sheet, turning each saucer over so the side which was up on the counter is down on the cookie sheet. If you have two cookie sheets you can bake six saucers at a time. Bake at 450 degrees for about five minutes, or until bread puffs up and is lightly browned.

While saucers bake, take the floured towels outside and shake off most of the flour. Spread them out again on your work surface. When saucers are done, remove cookie sheets from oven, using potholders or mitts, and with a pancake turner lift saucers onto the towels. Cover with the other two towels until saucers have cooled. Saucers will be puffed and hollow inside.

With a knife, make an opening in the side of each saucer. Stuff with tuna mix (Chapter 4) or egg mix (Chapter 4) or Unidentified Flyer mix (Chapter 8) or Galactic Goop (Chapter 2). *Makes 12 saucers.*

Astroriddle: Sometimes the natives of Jupiter's second moon act very wild. If you ask them to lunch, how can you keep them from pushing their bread saucers off the table? *Feed them on the floor.*

Astrofact: Two Project Voyagers were launched in 1977 to reach Jupiter in mid-1979. In the early 1980s, Galileo Mission will be launched, reaching Jupiter in 1984. Galileo will orbit Jupiter, drop probes into the atmosphere, then be flung by gravity-increased speed toward Saturn. One goal of this mission is a study of the Galileon satellites—Jupiter's four brightest moons—Io, Europa, Ganymede and Callisto, named by the early astronomer,

Galileo. We know of nine other satellites orbiting Jupiter, including the recently discovered Leda.

Astrotwister: Say the names of these satellites fast: Io, Europa, Ganymede and Callisto.

Astrofact: Jupiter's Galileon satellites—her four brightest moons—have thin atmosphere and lie within the planet's extreme and lethal radiation. Jupiter's largest moons are no more than 100 kilometers in diameter.

Callisto is the outermost of the four. It looks like dark rock, but does not have the density of rock, so it is believed to have large amounts of water on the surface.

Ganymede is formed of part dirt, part water, and it has more rock than Callisto.

Europa, the smallest, is coated with ice, giving it a bright, shiny appearance. Europa's density indicates that this satellite is mostly rock.

Io is rocky with the size and density of Earth's moon, but it appears to be covered by salt—as in the case of an evaporated sea bed.

Astroriddle: What did ten-year-old Mary find in the skillet when she tried cooking the strange vegetables on Jupiter's second moon? *Unidentified frying objects.*

JUPITER PUZZLE

Across:

1. Energy is normally produced by a star and _____ by planets.
4. Jupiter is the largest _____ planet in our solar system.
5. Scientists are making plans for colonies which may _____ be built in space.
6. To date, thirteen _____ or satellites have been discovered orbiting Jupiter.
7. Jupiter's four brightest moons were _____ by Galileo.

Down:

2. Some scientists believe Jupiter may be a _____.
3. Jupiter is the _____ to the outer planets.
5. The Great Red Spot of Jupiter is a raging _____.

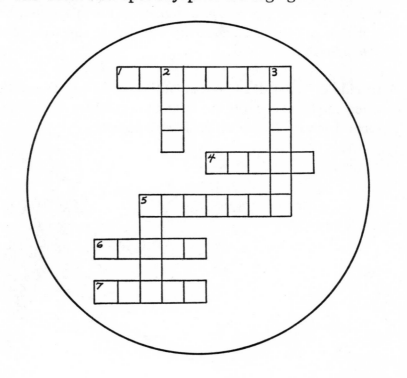

SATURN STACKUPS
Sandwiches

Sat-On Sandwiches

Lora was angry. She followed the rest of the crowd into the rocketport to wish Brill good luck, but she stayed angry.

"Brill again," she said to herself. "Always Brill getting the prizes and praise. They should ask why he doesn't spend more time with business and less time dreaming of inventions. That would take some answering."

But all the people from Lora and Brill's colony crowd seemed happy to cheer Brill on his way. "Good luck on Galactic Center," they cried. "Wow them with your new sandwich, Brill."

Sandwich, Lora thought bitterly, now it was sandwich. Last month it was the space pillow to cushion long voyages. Brill dreamed it up and put it together in a bright magna-zippered case and hurried off to Galactic Center to sell it. He did, too. He came home with a fat bundle of space credits for his idea.

Now Brill had put together a super sandwich he planned to sell to a fast-foods franchise in Galactic Center. Lora twisted her face in disgust. Some people said Brill's ideas put the space colony in the news. But Lora thought Brill used the ideas as an excuse to get away from the hard work of the colony.

She watched Brill set his fancy cushion and his super sandwich bag near the space lock, then go around shaking hands with everyone.

"Show off," Lora thought. Then she looked again at the two bags. They were almost the same size. An idea came to Lora. Both bags magna-zipped. Suppose . . . just suppose the cushion and sandwich were switched?

Brill was making a farewell speech. No one was looking at the two bags. It took Lora just an instant to zip them both open and switch the contents.

"Wait till Brill gets to Galactic Center and tries to sell them a pillow-sandwich," she told herself chuckling. "Wait till he finds he sat on his super sandwich all the way there!" It was hard to keep from laughing out loud at the thought.

At last Brill stopped making speeches and slipped into the shuttle. Lora smiled as Brill and the sandwich zoomed away. Then she walked with the rest of the crowd back to the farm and to work.

It was three Earth-days later when the newstape beamed into the colony. "SPACE COOK INVENTS SPACE-SAVING SANDWICH" read the headlines. Lora could hardly believe it. She bent over the tapes and read on.

"Brill XIV of Space Colony LX wowed Galactic Fast-Food Franchisers with his latest invention—a sandwich the space explorer can use as a cushion on his outer-space travels, then eat! Inventor Brill states, 'Sitting on the sandwich blends the flavors for full dining (and sitting) pleasure.'"

The newstape picture showed a very pleased Brill being awarded a trophy and a huge bundle of credits. If the camera had reversed and showed Space Colony LX, it would have photographed blank air. For Lora was sprawled on the floor bashing her hands and feet up and down in an old-fashioned Earth-style tantrum.

Astrofact: Saturn, a large planet which rotates fast, has 10 satellites. It takes so long for Saturn to orbit the sun that a year there is like 30 years on Earth. How many days would that be? (30 × 365) Saturn is a spectacularly ringed giant of a planet. The rings are 270,000 kilometers across but only one or two kilometers thick. That's like saying the rings are thinner than a piece of tissue paper compared to their width. Some scientists believe the rings are made of metal chunks, but most believe they are made of ice the size of snowballs and ice cubes.

☆ SAT-ON SANDWICH

Try Brill's cushion sandwich! Astrocooks who weigh 140 pounds *or less* sit on the wrapped sandwich long enough to crush olives and blend flavors.

1 large round loaf of French bread	*cutting board*
12 slices Monterey Jack or Cheddar cheese	*paring knife*
	tablespoon
	waxed paper
18 slices Italian dry salami	*table knife or spatula*
	strainer
1 green bell pepper	
2 cups ripe black olives, without pits	
butter or margarine, softened	

Pour olives into strainer and set aside to drain. Cut green pepper into rings. Clean out seeds and white pulp and discard.

Slice French loaf through the center, like a giant hamburger bun. Use a spoon to hollow out the top and bottom, but leave a thick layer of bread all around. (Save crumbs for casserole topping.) Use table knife or spatula to spread both halves of French loaf with softened butter or margarine.

Cover bottom half of French loaf with cheese slices, salami slices, and green pepper rings. Add the drained black olives and cover with the loaf top. Wrap carefully in waxed paper, then place on cutting board and let astrocook or crew member who weighs no more than 140 pounds sit on the sandwich. The olives will crush into the layers below and blend all flavors. Remove wrapping and cut the loaf into 6 or 8 pie-shaped wedges and serve. *Serves 6 to 8.*

Astroriddle: Why did the chicken fly across the street? *That was no chicken . . . that was a UFO!*

☆ UNIDENTIFIED FLYER

What's an unidentified flyer? A chopped chicken sandwich mixture.

1 cup leftover cooked chicken *or* canned chicken	*paring knife*
	cutting board
	measuring cup
2 tbsp chopped celery	*measuring spoons*
1 tbsp chopped onion	*mixing bowl*
1 tbsp chopped pickle or pickle relish	
mayonnaise	
bread or crackers	

Chop enough cooked or canned chicken to measure about one cup by putting chicken on cutting board and cutting through it with the knife until it is chopped into small pieces. (Remember to keep your fingers away from the blade.) Place in mixing bowl. Chop celery, onion, and pickle and add to chicken. Add two tablespoons mayonnaise and stir. Add more mayonnaise, one tablespoon at a time, to moisten the mixture well. Use as a sandwich spread on your favorite kind of bread or crackers. *Serves 4 to 6.*

Astroknock Knock: Who's there? UFO. UFO who? U F Only today to make Unidentified Flyer for the picnic.

Astroriddle: Why wasn't Ken worried when he stayed too long at an astromovie and missed the dinner-time shuttle rocket? *He knew he'd catch it when he got home.*

Astrofact: Titan, one of Saturn's moons, is known to have a major atmosphere that appears to be similar to the one which surrounded Earth long ago. The surface of Titan may contain the same type of molecules that existed on Earth when our planet was still in its primitive stage. Titan is larger than Mercury and veiled with clouds like Venus.

Astroriddle: What's as round as the moon and black as space? *An astrocook's iron skillet.*

Frankfurter strips curl like rocket flames when cooked in sauce.

4 frankfurters	*paring knife*
1 4-oz can of tomato sauce	*cutting board*
¼ cup water	*measuring cup*
¼ tsp dried oregano	*measuring spoons*
1 tsp Worcestershire sauce	*small skillet with lid*
4 hamburger buns	*mixing spoon*

Put franks on cutting board and use paring knife to cut them into long thin strips. You should get 4 to 6 strips from each frank, depending on size. Put the rest of the ingredients into the skillet and stir to blend. Put over medium heat until bubbles begin to form. Add frank strips and lower the heat. Cover to keep spatters from the stove. Simmer franks in sauce for 10 minutes. Spoon onto hamburger buns to serve. *Serves 4.*

Astrojoke:
Mother: Are you really going to take three pigs with you on the spaceship?
Son: Of course I am. I can't leave them here.
Mother: But what about the smell?
Son: Oh, the pigs won't mind.

☆ SPACE DIPS

Remember this when you have leftover roast beef.

1 cup roast beef *or* **6 oz beef cold cuts**	*paring knife*
	cutting board
2 tbsp butter or margarine	*saucepan*
1-oz package au jus mix from market spice rack	*measuring cup*
	mixing spoon
2 cups water	*skillet*
4 French rolls	*4 mugs*
	4 small plates

Combine au jus mix with 2 cups of water in saucepan. Stir well to blend. Put over medium heat and bring to a boil. Turn heat to low. Simmer, without a lid, for 5 minutes. Stir once in a while.

Cut the beef into thin slices. Melt margarine or butter in skillet. Put beef (or cold cuts) into skillet over low heat. Turn and cook until meat is warmed through.

Arrange heated meat in equal portions on four French rolls and place on small plates. Pour au jus into four mugs. Astroguests dip rolls into mugs to soak up au jus for each delicious bite. *Serves 4.*

Astroextra: Frank strips in tomato sauce make a surprise topping for cooked spaghetti!

Astrofact: Saturn's rings tilt along our line of view. The next view straight at the ring edge will be in 1980. Janus, the tenth moon of Saturn, was discovered in 1966, the last time the rings were edgewise toward Earth. Because Janus is so close to Saturn it won't be seen again until the edgewise view in 1980.

Astrotwister: Show me seven shipshape starships.

These unusual sandwiches won't get soggy on your way to the picnic.

1 cucumber *or* **1 apple and**	*paring knife*
lemon juice	*cutting board*
peanut butter	*vegetable peeler*
cream cheese	*table knife*

Peel cucumber with vegetable peeler. Slice into rounds about ¼ inch thick. Remove seeds from center of each round (Or slice apple into rounds about ¼ inch thick and cut out the core from the center of each round. Sprinkle apple rounds with lemon juice.)

Spread one cucumber round or one apple round with peanut butter, top with a second round and spread that one with cream cheese, top with a third round—and you have a Picnic Saucer.

or—spread both rounds with peanut butter.

or—spread both rounds with cream cheese.

Serves 1.

Astroriddle: What time is it when an ugly monster from outer space says, "Take me to your leader"? *It's time to take him to your leader—as fast as you can. After all, he might be hungry.*

Astroriddle: Where was the astrocook when the lights went out in the colony kitchen? *In the dark.*

☆ LEADER SANDWICH

This recipe makes enough to serve your entire crew—do-it-yourself style.

6 sandwich rolls
3 slices bologna
3 slices salami
3 slices Swiss cheese
1 small onion
pickles, sweet and dill
lettuce
mayonnaise
mustard
ketchup

paring knife
cutting board
serving plate

Cut bologna, salami, and cheese slices in half. Place one-half slice of each into a sandwich roll. (If rolls are not already sliced, cut each one in half lengthwise.) Peel and slice onion. Separate the slices into rings. Slice pickles. Place onion rings, pickles, and lettuce leaves on a serving plate, keeping the sweet pickles separate from the dills.

Give each member of the crew a sandwich roll with meat and cheese inside. Then pass the other ingredients so the crew can build their sandwiches just the way they like them. *Serves 6.*

☆ GALACTIC CHOICE

Open sandwiches with space-age toppings.

Breads: choose your favorite or use a few slices of each of these—whole wheat, pumpernickel, rye, or crisp cracker.

Spreads: butter or margarine.

Fillings: choose your favorites from these—cooked shrimp, onion rings, tomato slices, boiled egg slices, sweet pickles, black olives, green olives, cream cheese, sliced cheese, dill pickles, and so on. Place bread slices on serving tray. Spread with butter or margarine. Think of ways to arrange toppings in space-age patterns. Here are a few ideas to get you started.

1. Spread cream cheese on pumpernickel round. Cut black olive into wedges and arrange on cheese in the shape of a star.
2. An oval slice of rye bread can be a crowded shuttle rocket. Place cooked shrimp on slice for passengers. Put 3 or 4 onion rings or pimento-stuffed green olive slices across the shrimp for portholes.
3. Use star-shaped cookie cutter to cut through center of cold cut. (Save cut-out for No. 4.) Place slice with hole over square of bread. Fill hole with pickle relish or cheese from tube.
4. Place star cutout over crisp cracker or smaller bread round. Top with dab of relish and slice of pickle.
5. A tomato slice resembles a wheel or torus colony. Place it on a round or square bread slice. Top with "shuttle rocket"—a long dill slice or small whole gherkin.
6. Boiled egg slices look like suns or planets. Choose what you will add to them for flavor and a space-age look: a sweet pickle like a passing rocket, a salami slice to make an eclipse—or you can think of other ideas.

Astroriddles: When space colonists settle in wheel, or other, shape colonies between Earth and the moon, many will work on farms to raise food for the colony. See if you can answer these farm and garden riddles.

Why is a vegetable garden like a satellite diamond mine? *One has carrots, the other has carats.*

What fruit is like a planet with two moons? *A pear (pair).*
What vegetable is like a 10G liftoff? *Squash.*
What vegetable is like a hole in a wheel colony wall? *Leek (leak).*
What vegetable has more eyes than the farmer, yet cannot see? *Potato.*

☆ SUN AND MOONWICHES

Light and dark breads combine for a party sandwich.

2 slices dark wheat bread	*cutting board*
2 slices white bread	*star-shaped canape cutter*
sandwich filling (see	*table knife*
tip below)	

Put one slice of dark bread on cutting board. Use canape cutter to cut four stars from slice, one from each corner, but do not cut through crust. Be sure the cutter goes all the way through slice, so the bread doesn't tear when you push out the stars. Cut one slice of white bread in the same way.

Spread sandwich filling over the uncut slices of white and dark bread. Push the light-colored stars into the holes in the

111

dark bread. Push the dark-colored stars into the holes in the light bread. Place star-filled bread over sandwich spread. *Makes 2 uncut sandwiches* or *4 sandwich halves* or *8 party sandwich quarters.*
Filling Tips: Unidentified Flyer (Chapter 6)
              Planetary Peanut Butter (Chapter 6)
              Star Puff filling (Chapter 3)
              Galactic Goop (Chapter 2)
              Mars Salads II and III (Chapter 6)

Astroriddle: If two's company and three's a crowd, what are four and five? *Nine—just enough for Planetary Peanut Butter.*

☆ PLANETARY PEANUT BUTTER

Nine ways to use it in a sandwich.
1. Spread one slice of bread with peanut butter. Spread the other slice with mayonnaise.
2. To plain peanut butter sandwich or peanut butter/mayonnaise combination, add one tablespoon chopped onion.
3. Or add one tablespoon chopped celery.
4. Or add one tablespoon grated carrot.
5. Or add slices of avocado.
6. Or add a crunchy lettuce leaf.
7. Or add pickle slices.

8. Or add one tablespoon sliced or chopped olives.
9. Or for a gigantic galactic combination, make a sandwich with as many of the above ingredients as you like. Believe it or not, they all taste good together.

Astroriddle: Why was the little Saturnian strawberry sad? *Because his mother and father got into a jam.*

Astrofact: Long ago, only seven objects could be seen in the sky. These were the sun, the moon, Mars, Mercury, Jupiter, Venus, and Saturn. The seven days of the week were named for these seven objects (or for the gods and goddesses who were said to rule them). Thus, Saturday meant Saturn's Day.

Astroriddle: What did Mars and Jupiter whisper about Saturn? *"Ring around the planet."*

Astrofact: Voyagers I and II will pass Jupiter in 1979, then travel on to pass Saturn in November 1980 and August 1981, then travel on to Uranus. Voyager I will send back TV pictures of Titan and study the large moon for pressure, density, and chemical makeup. Voyager I will pass three more of Saturn's moons before leaving the area. Voyager II will pass three of Saturn's moons, but could be made to duplicate the earlier orbit, passing close to Titan, if more information on the giant moon is wanted.

SATURN PUZZLE

Across:

  2. Saturn's rings may be made of _____.

  6. Name of missions to pass Saturn in 1980 and 1981.

  8. Would we feel warm or cold near Saturn?

  9. Counting from the sun, Saturn is planet number _____.

11. What is Saturn best known for?

Down:

  1. Compared to their width, Saturn's rings are thinner than what Earth material? (two words)

  3. In 1980 our view of the rings will be of what surface?

  4. Saturn's largest moon.

  5. Titan and the planet Venus are hidden by what?

  7. Saturn has ten known _____.

10. Saturn's tenth moon, discovered in 1966.

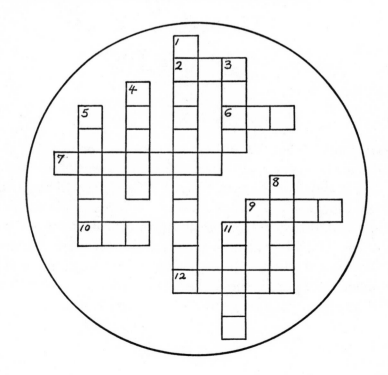

URANUS UNLIMITED
Desserts

Don't Take Souvenirs

When the space tour guide said, "No souvenirs," Merylee didn't think that meant ruby chips from the roadbed on Jewel II, or a crystalline water glass from the third moon of the planet Glitter. She poked them both in her traveling bag.

When the tour reached Cave Planet, it was the same story again. "No souvenirs," the guide said firmly. "Don't leave the group. Don't use heat-ray cameras. Don't touch the formations."

"Don't this . . . don't that," Merylee complained. "We paid good money for this trip. Why don't they let us relax and enjoy it?"

The deep-cave tour was almost interesting enough for Merylee to forget her complaints. Jewel-toned ribbon drapes curved along the walls. Stalactites gleamed from the ceiling. Chunky stalagmites grew up from the floor.

The guide made the tour visitors laugh when she pointed out how the stalagmites looked like storybook characters and many kinds of outer-spacers. She banged her walking stick on the stalagmites so the tourists could hear the stone ring like organ chimes.

"Don't touch," the guide reminded sharply when Merylee reached toward the shiny top of a stalagmite. Merylee pulled back her hand, but made a face when the guide couldn't see her.

The deepest room of the cave was lined with sparkly orange-brown rocks. More of the funny shaped stalagmites grew from the floor, but it was the rocks Merylee liked. "Wow," she thought, "wouldn't they make super souvenirs!"

"I am going to demonstrate total darkness," the guide said. "When I turn out the lights, you will not be able to see your hand in front of your eyes."

It was true. The lights went off, and Merylee stumbled off balance in the dark. Her hand struck one of the stalagmites. There was no warning from the guide. "Ha, ha, guide," Merylee thought. "You didn't see that, did you?"

She thought of something else at the same moment—the cave rocks. The guide couldn't see the rocks in the dark.

Merylee reached out quickly and pulled a rock from the cave wall. She stuffed it into her pocket. The rock felt strange to her touch. Kind of cold and clammy. It made Merylee feel cold and clammy, too. She wished the lights would come on again soon. Her feet were cold—they felt numb. She felt numb all over.

When the lights did come on, no one could find Merylee. No one noticed one more person-shaped stalagmite growing from the cave floor, a stalagmite with a cave rock stuck along one side.

The stalagmite did notice the people. It hoped, very

much, that the guide would not bang against it with that walking stick.

Astrofact: Uranus, with 5 satellites, is 1,783 million miles away from the sun.

☆☆ CAVE ROCKS

These candylike rocks are full of good things . . . and they won't turn you into a stalagmite.

1 cup golden seedless raisins	*cookie sheet*
1 cup dried apricots	*hot pad*
½ cup shredded coconut	*potholders and mitts*
1 cup whole almonds	*mixing spoon*
2 tbsp honey	*small saucepan with lid*
1 cup wheat germ *or* 1 cup ground sunflower seeds	*measuring cups and spoons*
	strainer
	food chopper or heavy knife and cutting board
	shallow bowl

Turn oven on to 350 degrees. Put raisins and apricots into a saucepan. Add just enough water to cover the fruit. Put a lid on the pan and place over medium heat. When you hear the water bubbling, turn heat to low. Let fruit simmer for about five minutes. Using potholder or mitt, remove lid carefully and pour fruit into strainer to drain.

While fruit simmers and drains, toast the coconut. Spread it out in a thin layer on a cookie sheet. Heat in the oven for about ten minutes, stirring now and then. When coconut is dry and toasty brown, remove cookie sheet from oven. Use potholders or mitts and set the cookie sheet on a hot pad to protect your work surface. Turn off the oven.

117

Now put the drained raisins and apricots and the almonds through a food chopper, using the medium blade. Or put the raisins, apricots, and almonds on a cutting board. Use heavy knife to cut through and through the mixture, taking care to keep your fingers away from the blade.

Place fruit, nuts, coconut, and honey into a bowl and mix well. Shape into chunky cave rocks about the size of a walnut. Roll each one in wheat germ or ground sunflower seeds, pressing firmly so all of the cave rock is well coated. Place rocks on cookie sheet covered with waxed paper. Place another piece of waxed paper over the rocks and let stand until dry. *Makes about 3 dozen.*

Astrofact: Uranus is almost four times the size of Earth, but because it is a gaseous planet, the surface gravity of Uranus is about the same as that of Earth.

☆☆ INNER SPACE COOKIES

These cookies taste delicious, and they're made with ingredients that are nourishing for your inner spaces, too.

butter or margarine	*cookie sheet*
¼ cup vegetable oil	*mixing bowl*
⅓ cup honey	*measuring cups and spoons*
½ cup peanut butter	*teaspoons*
¾ cup whole wheat flour	*mixing spoon*
¼ cup wheat germ	
½ tsp vanilla	
1 tsp baking powder	
¼ cup chopped nuts	
¼ cup sunflower seeds	
½ cup carob chips	
or raisins	

Using a small fold of waxed paper, grease cookie sheet with butter or margarine. Turn oven on to 325 degrees.

Place oil, honey, and peanut butter into mixing bowl. (Measure oil first, then use the same cup to measure the honey, and last, the peanut butter. There is no need to wash the cup in between each of these measurements.) Mix these ingredients well. Add flour, wheat germ, vanilla, and baking powder. Mix again. Add nuts, sunflower seeds, carob chips or raisins, and stir until dough is well mixed.

Dip a teaspoon of dough (not a measuring teaspoon, but the kind you use when setting the dinner table) and using your finger or another spoon, scrape the dough off and let it drop onto a greased cookie sheet. Drop cookies into rows about ½ inch apart each way. Bake at 325 degrees about 12 minutes, or until firm and lightly browned. *Makes 3 to 4 dozen.*

Astrotip: If you don't have nuts *and* sunflower seeds *and* carob chips or raisins, these ingredients together add up to one cup. So you can use one cup of nuts or one cup of raisins or one cup of carob chips or ⅓ cup of each—or any combination of these ingredients that adds up to one cup.

Astroriddle: Why did the Uranian jelly roll? *It saw the Venusian apple turnover.*

Astrofact: Asteroids have sometimes been called "cosmic cannonballs."

Astrotwister: Say this fast several times. Robbie's bumbling robot fumbles footballs.

☆☆ COSMIC COOKIES

Cosmos comes from a Greek word for universe and order. Cosmic Cookies contain a variety of ingredients baked together in yummy order.

½ cup butter or margarine   *measuring cups and spoons*
1 cup brown sugar   *mixing spoon*
1 cup cottage cheese   *electric mixer*
⅓ cup peanut butter   *large mixer bowl*
1 egg   *flour sifter*
1 tsp vanilla   *waxed paper*
1 cup whole wheat flour   *cookie sheets*
¼ tsp baking soda   *hot pads or mitts*
baking powder
1 tsp salt
1 tsp cinnamon
1 cup oatmeal
¾ cup chopped walnuts
¾ cup raisins

Using a small fold of waxed paper, grease cookie sheets with butter or margarine. Put butter or margarine and sugar in large mixing bowl and beat with electric mixer (or by hand) until creamy, then stop mixer. (If you've never used a mixer before, ask an adult for directions.)

Add cottage cheese, peanut butter, egg, and vanilla to mixture in bowl and beat until well blended. Rinse mixer blades or drop them into a pan of hot soapy water to soak.

Heat oven to 350 degrees. Set flour sifter on piece of waxed paper. Put flour, baking soda, baking powder, salt, and cinnamon into the sifter and sift ingredients onto paper. Then lift paper carefully and pour the dry ingredients into cottage cheese mixture. Add oatmeal, walnuts, and raisins and stir until well blended.

Drop dough by teaspoonfuls onto sheets in rows about 1

inch apart. Bake at 350 degrees for about 10 minutes. *Makes 6 dozen.*

Astroriddle: Which is the left part of a Uranian dessert? *The part that's not eaten is the one that's left.*

Astrofact: Planet means wandering star, because scientists originally believed that stars did not move. They believed planets were bodies of matter that moved around stars which always stayed in the same location. But now we know that stars, including our own sun, are also moving through the sky.

☆ CREAMY PLANETS

Choose your favorite ice cream flavors and colors for a galaxy of ringed planets.

ice cream, firmly frozen
large flat cookies

ice cream scoop
sharp knife
cutting board
shallow pan
waxed paper
serving dishes

For each serving, use scoop to make firm round ice cream ball. Cut each ball in half through the middle. Place cut side down on shallow pan. Cover ice cream with sheet of waxed paper and place pan in freezer. Chill serving dishes in refrigerator.

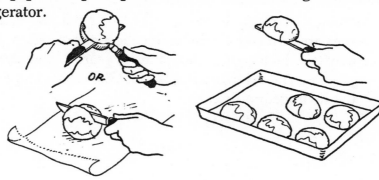

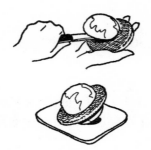

When ready to serve, remove dishes and tray of ice cream to work table. Put the halved ice cream balls back together with a flat cookie between the halves. The cookie should be larger than the ball of ice cream so it will show around the sides.

Place on chilled serving dishes, tilting each ice cream planet so the cookie "ring" touches the dish on one side, aims upward on the other.

Serve at once or freeze until party time.

Solar Riddles: What sun do you have to polish off when you clean your rocket? *Sunspot.*

What sun is a dessert on Pluto? *Sundae.*

What sun can a space colonist use to build a house? *Sunbeam.*

What sun do colonists take for walks? *Sundog.*

What sun do you need if you fall into a sea on Earth? *Sunstroke.*

What sun does an astronaut need to walk on the day side of Uranus? *Sunsuit.*

What sun does an astrocook keep out of the cookpot? *Sunburn.*

Astrofact: Stars come and go. Scientists believe that new stars are formed by nebulas or collections of gasses. But it may take hundreds of thousands of years to complete the process. The death of a star begins when it has lost most of the hydrogen in its core.

☆☆ PLUTO PARTY POPS

Icy fruit desserts to make ahead and pop out for parties. Use pineapple *or* strawberries, and vanilla *or* almond flavoring.

2 cups buttermilk	*measuring cups*
1 can (1 lb 4 oz) crushed	*measuring spoons*
pineapple with juice	*large bowl*
or 10-oz package frozen	*small mixer bowl*
strawberries	*electric mixer*
½ tsp vanilla *or*	*mixing spoon*
almond flavoring	*8 6-oz paper cups*
½ cup honey	*8 popsickle sticks*
2 egg whites	

To separate eggs, have the small electric mixer bowl ready for the whites. Have a smaller bowl ready for the yolks. Wash your hands thoroughly. Break one egg at a time into your hand, holding your fingers almost closed so the white runs through into the bowl and the yolk stays unbroken on your palm. Slide the yolk into the small bowl. Repeat with the second egg.

Astrotip: Cover the yolks with milk so they won't dry out. Store in refrigerator to use for French toast or scrambled eggs.

Use electric mixer (if it's your first time, ask an adult to help) to beat egg whites until they form soft peaks when you stop the mixer and lift the blades from the bowl. Remove from mixer and set aside.

Put buttermilk, pineapple with juice from can, (or thawed strawberries and juice) honey, and vanilla or almond flavoring into large mixing bowl. Stir until well blended. Spoon beaten egg whites into buttermilk mixture. Gently *fold* whites into mixture by dipping spoon through the whites under the mixture and up through the center. Repeat until the whites are well mixed in.

Set out 8 6-ounce paper cups. Use another paper cup as a dipper to fill the cups with the buttermilk mixture. Place cups in a shallow pan and set in freezer. When mixture is partially frozen, poke a popsickle stick into the center of each party pop. Continue freezing until firm.

To serve, remove pan from freezer and allow pops to stand at room temperature a few minutes, until they just barely begin to thaw around the edge. Then you will be able to place your fingers on top of the cup, thumbs on the bottom, and pop out your party pop. *Serves 8.*

Astroriddle: Using just three letters, can you spell the favorite water dessert on Pluto? *Ice.*

☆ STARSHINE ICE CREAM

Quick sparkle to make party ice cream starshine bright.

1 3-oz package strawberry gelatin	*medium bowl*
1¼ cups water	*measuring cup*
½ cup cold water	*mixing spoon*
vanilla ice cream	*8-inch square baking pan*
	paring knife
	serving dishes

Put gelatin into bowl. Put 1¼ cups water into small saucepan, cover, and bring water to a boil. Measure 1 cup of boiling water and add to gelatin. (Younger astrocooks should ask an adult for help with boiling water.) Stir until gelatin dissolves. Stir in ½ cup cold water. Pour into thin layer in bottom of baking pan. Chill in refrigerator until firm.

When gelatin is firm, remove from refrigerator. Use paring knife to slice gelatin into tiny squares. Spoon ice cream into serving dishes. Sprinkle sparkly bits of starshine gelatin over the top. *Tops 8 or more servings.*

☆ SOLAR WHIP

Your entire crew will enjoy this sunshine-bright dessert.

1 cup orange juice
1 3-oz package orange gelatin
1 banana *or* small can mandarin orange slices
plain yogurt
chopped nuts

small saucepan with lid
potholders or mitts
bowl
measuring cup
mixing spoon
can opener (if using orange slices)
eggbeater
hot pad
tablespoon
four glasses, dessert dishes, or small bowls

Squeeze enough oranges to make one cup of juice, or mix a quart of frozen orange juice. Chill in refrigerator.

In small saucepan, bring 1¼ cups of water to a boil. (To save energy, use a lid on the pan—the water will boil more quickly.) Empty contents of gelatin package into mixing bowl. Using potholders or mitts, measure out one cup of

125

boiling water. (Younger astrocooks should ask for help.) Pour water over gelatin and stir until thoroughly dissolved.

Stir in 1 cup chilled orange juice. Place mixture in refrigerator for about 30 minutes, or until it is just beginning to jell but is not quite firm.

Now, place the bowl of gelatin on a hot pad or towel (so it won't slip) on your work surface. With an eggbeater, whip the gelatin until it's light and frothy.

Return it to the refrigerator for five minutes. Peel and slice the banana or open a can of mandarin oranges.

Remove the fluffy gelatin from the refrigerator and spoon a layer one or two inches deep into the bottom of a drinking glass, dessert dish, or small bowl. Add a few slices of banana or orange and another layer of gelatin.

Repeat until all fruit and gelatin have been used, ending with a layer of gelatin on top. Return the Solar Whip to the refrigerator to chill well before serving.

For special occasions, top the whip with a swirl of plain yogurt sprinkled with chopped nuts. *Serves 4.*

Astrofact: A day on the moon is as long as two weeks on Earth. During the day, the temperature may go as high as 212 degrees. During the long lunar night, the temperature goes as low as 240 degrees below zero.

☆ LUNAR WHIP

A cool dessert, but not as cold as a night on the moon.

1 cup pineapple juice	*small saucepan with lid*
1 3-oz package lemon	*potholders or mitts*
gelatin	*bowl*
1 banana *or* 1 peach *or*	*measuring cup*
1 pear *or* 1 bunch of	*mixing spoon*
grapes	*can opener*
plain yogurt	*egg beater*
chopped nuts	*hot pad*
	tablespoon
	four glasses, dessert
	dishes, or small bowls

Chill a can of pineapple juice.

In small saucepan, bring 1¼ cups of water to a boil. Empty contents of gelatin package into mixing bowl. Using potholders or mitts, measure out one cup of boiling water. (Younger astrocooks should ask for help.) Pour water over gelatin and stir until thoroughly dissolved.

Stir in 1 cup chilled pineapple juice. Place mixture in refrigerator for about thirty minutes, or until it is just beginning to jell but is not quite firm.

Now, place the bowl of gelatin on a hot pad or towel (so it won't slip) on your work surface. With an eggbeater, whip the gelatin until it's light and frothy.

Return it to the refrigerator for five minutes. Peel and slice the banana, peach, or pear—or wash and dry the grapes and remove all stems.

Take the fluffy gelatin from the refrigerator and spoon a layer one or two inches deep into the bottom of a drinking glass, dessert dish, or small bowl. Add a few slices of fruit and another layer of gelatin. Repeat until all fruit and gelatin have been used, ending with a layer of gelatin on top. Return the Lunar Whip to the refrigerator to chill well before serving.

If you like, top the whip with a swirl of plain yogurt and a sprinkle of chopped nuts. *Serves 4.*

Astroriddle: How can you pick fruit from a nectar tree on Mars with out disturbing the dangerous swordbird who lives there? *Wait until the bird flies away.*

☆ MARS WHIP

Whether your guests are Martians or Earthlings, they're sure to like this light dessert.

1 cup apple juice	*small saucepan with lid*
1 3-oz package cherry gelatin	*potholders or mitts*
	bowl
1 basket fresh berries *or*	*measuring cup*
1 package frozen berries	*mixing spoon*
plain yogurt	*can opener*
chopped nuts	*eggbeater*
	hot pad
	tablespoon
	four glasses, dessert dishes, or small bowls

Chill a can of apple juice. Remove hulls and wash fresh berries, or take frozen berries from freezer so they can begin to thaw.

In small saucepan, bring 1¼ cups of water to a boil. Empty contents of gelatin package into mixing bowl. Using potholders or mitts, measure out one cup of boiling water. (Younger astrocooks should ask for help.) Pour water over gelatin and stir until thoroughly dissolved.

128

Stir in 1 cup chilled apple juice. Place mixture in refrigerator for about thirty minutes, or until it is just beginning to jell but not quite firm.

Now, place the bowl of gelatin on a hot pad or towel (so it won't slip) on your work surface. With an eggbeater, whip the gelatin until it's light and frothy.

Return the bowl to the refrigerator for five minutes, then bring it back to your work surface. Spoon a layer of gelatin about one or two inches deep into the bottom of a drinking glass, dessert dish, or small bowl. Add a few berries and another layer of gelatin. Repeat until all fruit and gelatin have been used, ending with a layer of gelatin. Return the Mars Whip to the refrigerator to chill well before serving.

For a special touch, top the whip with a swirl of plain yogurt and a sprinkle of chopped nuts. *Serves 4.*

Astroextra: Now that you've got the whip idea, make up one of your own. Try grapefruit juice with lime gelatin, cranapple juice with apple gelatin, or grape juice with grape gelatin.

Astroknock Knock: Who's there? Terra. Terra who? Terra flies in my Starshine Ice Cream!

Astrofact: A white dwarf is a shining white star that is losing hydrogen and shrinking. As it becomes even smaller, and the white light fades, it is called a black dwarf.

☆ MARSHMALLOW ROBOTS

This is a party favor and dessert all in one.

marshmallows, large and small
food coloring
clean hands

toothpicks
kitchen scissors
imagination

On a clean work surface, assemble a bag of large marsh-mallows, a bag of small marshmallows, a box of toothpicks, kitchen scissors, and a small food coloring kit. Now you are ready to design the most imaginative robots ever seen in this universe.

Use toothpicks, or pieces of toothpicks, to join large and small marshmallows or pieces of large marshmallows which have been cut in half lengthwise, crosswise, or diagonally. In some cases you may want to leave the tip of the toothpick showing, to resemble a bolt or rivet. Dials, controls, and other markings can be added with food coloring applied with the tip of a toothpick.

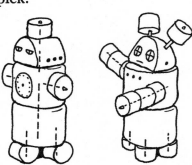

Astroriddle: If the astrocook went after wild turkeys roosting in an apple tree on Triton and shot one out of a flock of five, how many would be left? *None—the other four would fly away.*

☆ APPLESAUCER SAUCE

6 to 8 apples	*vegetable peeler*
cinnamon	*paring knife*
honey	*large saucepan with lid*
water	*cutting board*
	potholders or mitts
	potato masher or fork

Wash and peel the apples, cut in quarters, then cut away the core. Place in saucepan with about ¼ cup of water, cover, and cook over low heat until tender when tested with a fork. Check now and then to make sure water has not boiled away. You may need to add one or two tablespoons more.

When apples are tender, sprinkle lightly with cinnamon and mash with fork or potato masher. Allow the sauce to cool enough so you can taste it. If it is not quite sweet enough, stir in about 1 teaspoon honey. *Serves 4.*

Serve warm in the winter or cold in the summer—or use to fill Applesaucers (see recipe).

Astrofact: Uranus is a large planet surrounded by a dense greenish atmosphere and five moons. We believe Uranus has a rocky core and a thick shell of ice surrounded by gasses.

☆☆ STAR PASTRY

⅔ cup butter or margarine	*small saucepan with lid*
½ cup water	*fork*
2 cups flour	*mixing bowl*
½ tsp baking powder	*measuring cups and spoons*
½ tsp salt	*waxed paper*
	rolling pin

Place butter or margarine into mixing bowl about an hour before you are ready to make the pastry.

When ready to begin, bring ½ cup of water to a boil in small saucepan. (To save energy, use a lid—the water will boil more quickly.)

Measure ⅓ cup of boiling water (younger astrocooks should ask an adult to help) and pour over butter or margarine. Stir with a fork until mixture is creamy. Sprinkle flour over butter mixture, then sprinkle baking powder and salt over flour. Mix well with a fork. Pat dough into a ball, cover bowl, and chill in the refrigerator for about one hour.

Use for Applesaucers (see next recipe) or roll out and fill with your favorite pie filling, or roll out and bake, then fill with your favorite unbaked pie filling.

Before you roll out pastry, tear off two squares of waxed paper. Cut ball of pastry dough in half and place one piece of waxed paper on your work surface. Roll one section of dough into a ball and place it in the center of the waxed paper. Flatten the ball with your hands. Cover the flattened ball of dough with the second square of waxed paper. Use the rolling pin to roll out the dough until it is about 10 inches in diameter, then peel off top piece of waxed paper. Pick up the bottom piece of waxed paper with the dough on it and turn it upside down over a 9-inch pie plate. Then peel paper off the dough.

Repeat the process to make a second pie shell or a top crust.

To bake an empty pie shell, make holes in the dough with a fork, after placing dough in the pie plate. Prick all the way around the sides and bottom so the shell won't get bubbly while it bakes. Preheat oven to 425 degrees and bake for 10 to 15 minutes until the crust is golden brown. *Makes 2 pie shells.*

Astroknock Knock: Who's there? Saturn. Saturn who? You just saturn my Applesaucers! Please get up and go sit on my Sat-On Sandwich.

☆☆ APPLESAUCERS

These don't fly in the sky but they're yummy in the tummy.

1 recipe Star Pastry　　　　*cookie sheet*
1 recipe Applesaucer Sauce　*drinking glass*
cinnamon　　　　　　　　　*waxed paper*
butter or margarine　　　　*rolling pin*
　　　　　　　　　　　　　　fork
　　　　　　　　　　　　　　spatula
　　　　　　　　　　　　　　measuring spoons

Make Star Pastry and place in refrigerator to chill. Make Applesaucer Sauce and set aside. Assemble the rest of the ingredients and utensils listed above.

With a small fold of waxed paper, grease cookie sheet with butter or margarine. Tear off two large squares of waxed paper and place one on work surface. Flatten one ball of pastry dough in the center of the first piece of waxed paper, then cover dough with the second piece of waxed paper. Use rolling pin to roll dough into a 10 inch circle.

Using the end of a drinking glass, cut dough into smaller circles. With a spatula, carefully lift the circles from the waxed paper and place on greased cookie sheet. (Set scraps of dough aside.) Turn oven on to 450 degrees.

Place about 2 tablespoons of Applesaucer Sauce on the center of each pastry circle. Sprinkle sauce lightly with cinnamon.

Roll out the second ball of dough and cut into circles with drinking glass. Place one of these circles over each Applesaucer on the cookie sheet, then press the two circles of dough on each Applesaucer together with the fork. Also use the fork to poke an X on top of each Applesaucer. Again, sprinkle each one lightly with cinnamon. Each saucer will look like this.

Bake at 450 degrees for 15 to 20 minutes, or until lightly browned. Serve hot or cold. *Makes approximately 10.*

☆☆ BAKED PLANETS

This is an ideal winter dessert.

butter or margarine	*baking pan*
firm apples, either red or	*vegetable peeler and corer*
yellow or green	*small spoon*
raisins	
chopped nuts	
honey	
cinnamon	

With a small fold of waxed paper, grease the inside of a round, square, or oblong baking pan. Turn oven on to 350 degrees. Allow one apple for each member of the crew.

Cut out core, then peel skin off only the top inch of each apple. Stand the apple in a greased baking dish. Fill the core with raisins or a mixture of raisins and chopped nuts. With a small spoon, drizzle honey into the core so it runs down over the raisins and nuts. Lightly sprinkle the peeled top of each apple with cinnamon.

Bake at 350 degrees until apples feel tender when tested with a fork. (Some apples bake much more quickly than others. It may take from thirty minutes to an hour.) Serve either warm or cold, but on a wintry day, the warmer the better.

Astroextra: While Applesaucers bake, squeeze scraps of dough together to form a ball. Roll out between sheets of waxed paper. Cut into 2-inch squares. Sprinkle with brown sugar and cinnamon, or grated cheese. Bake at 450 degrees for about 12 minutes or until lightly browned.

Astrotip: Many times the simplest things are also the best. One of the best desserts is a platter of fresh fruits and sliced cheese arranged in an attractive design.

Astroriddle: What has eight legs, a shiny shell, and flies? *Four astronauts in a shiny spaceship.*

Astroknock Knock: Who's there? Planet. Planet who? Are you planet to wake up for dessert?

☆☆ SUPER GREEN SPACESHIP SUPREME

This concoction becomes a dessert and table decoration all in one.

1 bunch of seedless grapes
1 chilled watermelon
1 chilled cantaloupe

knife
cutting board
measuring spoons or
  melon ball scoop
large mixing bowl
serving platter

Wash and dry grapes, remove stems, then set grapes aside.

Check to see if your watermelon has one side which is slightly flat. This will be the bottom of the spaceship. If it does not have a flat side, ask an adult to slice off one side of the melon like this.

Then it can be placed on a flat surface without rolling. (This should be done only by an adult or an older astrocook, because the watermelon is slippery and may roll, causing you to lose control of the knife. Also, it is important *not* to cut all the way through to the flesh of the melon.)

Next cut an oval lid out of the top of the melon, so it looks like this.

(Younger cooks will need help with this step also.) Set aside the piece that you cut out—you will use it later.

With a tablespoon from your set of measuring spoons, or with a melon ball scoop, scoop out rounded chunks of watermelon, discarding all seeds. Continue scooping until you have removed all the pink fruit. Place the watermelon

136

balls into the large bowl as you scoop them out. Then place
the empty shell on a serving platter.

Now, on a cutting board, slice the cantaloupe in half, and
scrape out the seeds. With the tablespoon or melon ball
scoop, scoop out small rounds of cantaloupe and put them
into the mixing bowl with the watermelon balls. Add grapes
and stir gently to mix the three fruits well.

Place the lid which you cut from the watermelon on the
cutting board next, and slice it into strips and squares and
diamond shapes. These you can attach to the watermelon
shell with toothpicks, to make it resemble a spaceship. You
might want to cut the lid into two long strips, two triangles,
and eight small squares, like this.

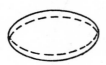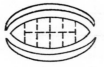

Then the finished ship might look like this.
Or use your own ideas.

Finally, using the largest spoon you have, spoon the
melon balls and grapes back into the watermelon shell.
Cover the opening with plastic wrap and refrigerate until
ready to serve. *Serves 12 or more.*

URANUS PUZZLE

Down:

1. A white _____ and a black _____ are names for different kinds of stars.
2. Asteroids (planetoids) have sometimes been called "cosmic _____."
5. How many satellites have been seen orbiting Uranus?
6. A day on the moon is as long as two _____ on Earth.
7. Planet means wandering _____.

Across:

3. _____ is about four times the size of Earth.
4. A lunar _____ is two weeks long.
8. Uranus is surrounded by a dense cold _____.

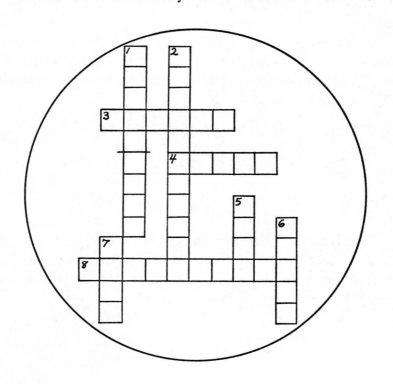

NEPTUNE NIBBLES
Snacks

Say What You Mean

"**R**emember, dear," Leana's father said, "your new robot will do just what you tell him."

"He'd better!" Leana said, then she smiled. It was not a pleasant smile. "I'm going to have a party. I'm the first girl on this forgotten satellite to have my own robot. Everyone is going to be so jealous!"

Leana's parents were space pilots. They were away from home a lot and often brought her gifts to make up for it. That was why her father brought the Butler Robot from his trip to Earth.

At Leana's words, her parents looked at each other with troubled frowns. Then her mother smiled and held out a box. "A party will be wonderful, dear. See what I've brought from Neptune for you to share with your friends."

Leana ripped open the box. "Neptune Nibbler?" she cried. "Oh, Mother, this will make everyone really jealous!"

She hugged her parents, then hurried to her room to plan the party.

Neptune Nibbles were rare. On that far and icy planet, the people sold the snacks only once every ten years. They prepared Neptune Nibblefruit with flavored ice and sealed it in porcelain cases. When you broke the case and let the icy fruit melt in your mouth, it tasted like a perfect blend of the best flavors in the entire universe.

"My friends will turn green with jealousy when *my* robot carries in *my* tray of Neptune Nibbles," Leana told herself smugly.

Then she thought again. "Why should I share the Neptune Nibbles with my friends? They're lucky just to be invited to my party. Why should they eat all the Neptune Nibbles as well?"

Leana handed the box to her robot. "I want you to hide the Neptune Nibbles," she said. But where would they be safe? If her parents found the Nibbles, they would say Leana was selfish. They wouldn't understand she was being thrifty and making the fruit last longer.

"Take them outside, she told the robot. She tapped a porcelain case with her fingernail. The case felt strong. "Bury the Nibblefruit in the sand," she said.

"I will bury the Nibblefruit in the sand," the robot repeated, then rolled from the room.

"Stupid creature," Leana told herself, "but he's enough to make the others jealous." She smiled again.

Leana had almost finished her invitations when the robot rolled in. His wheels and joints squeaked with sand as he rolled to Leana.

"Well, stupid," she said, "did you hide the Neptune Nibbles?"

"I buried the Nibblefruit in the sand as ordered," the robot said, his voice sounding rusty. Then he swung his arm around and held out a tray of broken porcelain cases. "What shall I do with the shells?"

Astrofact: On Neptune a year is as long as 165 days on Earth. This greenish-colored planet has two satellites, one large and one small. Uranus, Neptune, and Pluto are called the outer planets. Neptune, like Uranus, is about four times the size of Earth. Both are cold planets—so far away we don't know much about them. They are believed to be gaseous giants like Saturn and Jupiter.

☆ NEPTUNE SLURPIES

Leana's Neptune Nibbles call for rare frozen fruit. You can make Neptune Slurpies by freezing Earth fruit juices.

**your favorite fruit juice
(orange or lemonade or
fruit punch or
pineapple or any-
thing you like)**

ice cube trays
toothpicks

Pour fruit juice into ice cube trays and place in freezer. Check the juice after about an hour. When it begins to freeze, push toothpicks into each cube for handles. When the juice is frozen hard, pop the cubes from the trays. Hold by toothpick handles to eat.

Astroextra: Neptune Slurpies make party-special frozen cubes to add to cold punch or other cold beverage. Freeze without toothpicks. When frozen, pop the cubes from the ice cube trays, place in plastic bags, fasten with wire twistees, and freeze until needed.

Astrotip: Fresh chilled raw fruits and vegetables, just the way they come to us from good old planet Earth, are the quickest, easiest, most nutritious snacks of all.

☆ SPACE QUICK DONUTS

Count down the minutes for these quick and easy donuts.

butter or margarine
1 package refrigerated
  biscuits
cinnamon
honey

cookie sheet
waxed paper
potholders or mitts

With a small fold of waxed paper, grease a cookie sheet with butter or margarine. Turn oven on to 450 degrees. Open package of biscuits. With clean hands and fingernails, poke a hole in the center of each biscuit. *Gently* stretch the circle of dough until it resembles a donut. Try not to stretch so far the circle breaks, but if it does, simply mash the two ends together again.

Place the donuts about one inch apart on greased cookie sheet. Sprinkle lightly with cinnamon. Bake at 450 degrees for 8 to 10 minutes, or until lightly browned. Serve warm with butter or margarine and honey. *Makes 10.*

Astrofact: Asteroids are also called planetoids or minor planets. They are bodies of matter smaller than planets and may be bits remaining from an exploded planet. A belt of asteroids is located between the orbits of Mars and

Jupiter. Astronomers believe one of these, Herculina, has a satellite (or moon) traveling with it.

☆☆ METEOR MOUNDS

When a small object from space enters our atmosphere, it burns in a blaze of light called a meteor. Meteor Mounds are cold instead of hot, but they disappear almost as quickly with a hungry crew.

butter or margarine	*cookie sheet*
8 graham crackers	*mixing spoon*
½ cup nuts or sunflower	*rolling pin*
seeds (or ¼ cup each)	*cutting board*
¾ cup peanut butter	*skillet or saucepan*
⅔ cup honey	*paring knife*
¼ cup milk	*toothpicks*
4 bananas	*spatula or table knife*
	waxed paper

Use a small fold of waxed paper to grease a cookie sheet with butter or margarine. Place graham crackers in a folded sheet of waxed paper, put it on the cutting board, and use the back of the mixing spoon or the rolling pin to crumble the crackers. You need about 1½ cups of graham cracker crumbs. Place crumbs, nuts and/or sunflower seeds, peanut butter, honey, and milk into skillet or saucepan. Set aside.

Peel bananas. Cut into chunks about two inches long. Push a toothpick into each chunk. Place on greased cookie sheet and chill in the refrigerator.

Now stir all the ingredients in the skillet or saucepan. Place on stove over low heat and stir constantly just until peanut butter and honey are thoroughly melted and well mixed with the other ingredients. Turn off heat and leave pan on the warm burner.

Take banana chunks from refrigerator. Dip each one into the peanut butter mixture. Use a spatula or knife to coat the banana well with the mixture. Return each dipped banana chunk to the cookie sheet. When all the chunks have been dipped, cover the cookie sheet with plastic wrap and chill thirty minutes in the freezer before serving.

If you crew is small and you don't eat all the Meteor Mounds right away, wrap each of the extra ones in a piece of plastic wrap. Secure with a wire twistee and freeze. *Serves 4 to 6.*

Astroriddle: What time is it when you see a huge meteorite moving toward you? *Time to get out of the way!*

Astrojoke:
  Space Colony Chef: You have just one day to prepare snacks for the festival.
  Lazy helper: Okay. I choose one day next year.

Astroriddle: Dan and Cindy are planning a hyperspace jump to Aldebaran to pick bramble berries for Solar Fruit Strips. How far into hyperspace can they go? *Halfway— after that, they'll be coming out.*

SOLAR FRUIT STRIPS

Follow the recipes below to cook and mash fruit for these tangy strips. Directions for drying the fruit sauce in the oven or in the hot sun follow the recipes.

☆☆ APRICOT SOLAR STRIPS

1 cup chopped apricots
1½ tbsp honey

knife
measuring cup
measuring spoons
saucepan
potato masher
candy thermometer
blender or food mill and
*   wire strainer and heavy*
*   spoon*
cookie sheet
plastic wrap

Use ripe apricots. Cut away any bad spots, then cut apricots into small pieces and measure to make 1 cup. Put in saucepan with honey and crush with a potato masher while heating to 180 degrees. Let fruit cool to lukewarm.

Younger astrocooks should put fruit through food mill, then use a heavy spoon to force as much as possible through a wire strainer. Older astrocooks should ask permission to puree the fruit in a blender.

Follow directions below for drying fruit sauce in the oven or hot sun.

☆ STRAWBERRY SOLAR STRIPS

1 cup strawberries
1 tbsp honey

knife
measuring cup
measuring spoon
saucepan with lid
food mill and wire
*   strainer*
heavy spoon

Remove stems and wash berries. Measure to make 1 cup. Place in saucepan with honey, cover with lid, then put over medium heat and bring to a full rolling boil. Turn off heat and let fruit cool to lukewarm

Put berries through food mill, then use a heavy spoon to force fruit through a wire strainer. Follow directions below for drying fruit sauce in the oven or in hot sun.

Oven Drying: Line a jelly roll pan or other shallow tray with a strip of plastic wrap. Pour the fruit sauce over the plastic in a thin even layer. Spread with a rubber spatula. Heat the oven to a warm setting (140 to 150 degrees). Put in the trays and leave the oven door slightly open while the fruit dries. It will take about 8 to 10 hours. The fruit is ready when it doesn't feel sticky to your touch and it can be pulled from the plastic wrap. Roll it in the plastic like a jelly roll. It will keep in the refrigerator for 4 months.

☆☆ PLUM SOLAR STRIPS

1 cup chopped ripe plums
1½ tbsp honey
1 tbsp fresh orange juice

knife
measuring cup
measuring spoon
saucepan
potato masher
candy thermometer
blender or *food mill and wire strainer and heavy spoon*
cookie sheet
plastic wrap

Wash plums, then pat dry with paper towel. Cut into small pieces and measure to make 1 cup. Place in saucepan with orange juice and honey and crush with a potato masher while heating over low heat to 180 degrees. Turn off heat and cool to lukewarm.

Young astrocooks should put fruit through food mill, then force as much as possible through a wire strainer. Older astrocooks should ask permission to puree the fruit in a blender.

Follow directions below for drying fruit sauce in the oven or hot sun.

Sun Drying: Cover a small table with plastic wrap. Tape the ends under the edge so the plastic won't blow. Pour the prepared fruit sauce in a thin layer over the plastic. Be sure the sun shines on the table all day. A thin layer will dry in very hot sun in one day. If the layer is thicker or if the sun is not hot enough to finish drying the fruit in one day, slip a cookie sheet under the plastic and fruit and bring it into the house at night. Finish drying in the sun the next day or in the oven as described above.

If flies are a problem, place strips of wood along two sides of the table. Stretch a layer of cheesecloth above the fruit sauce and fasten it securely to the wood strips. Be sure the cloth does not touch the fruit. Let the ends of the cheese cloth hang down over the two open sides, so the fruit is protected all the way around.

When the fruit feels dry to your touch and can be peeled away from the plastic, it's ready to eat. Roll it in the plastic like a jelly roll. It will keep in the refrigerator for 4 months.

Astroriddle: Why did the entire crew of the Earthship walk out of the snack bar on Neptune? *They had just finished eating.*

Astrofact: The Solar Wind is a stream of atoms and charged particles constantly set forth in all directions by the sun. Solar Wind consists mainly of protons and electrons.

SOLAR DEBRIS

How to toast your own almonds, walnuts, or sunflower seeds.

☆ SOLAR ALMONDS

almonds	*sieve*
water	*saucepan with lid*
salt	*cookie sheet*
	potholders or mitts

Blanch shelled nuts: fill a saucepan half full of water, cover with lid, place on medium heat, and bring to a boil. Put shelled nuts in a sieve and lower the sieve into boiling water for a few seconds. (Younger astrocooks should ask an adult to help.) Lift out and pour nuts onto cookie sheet. Squeeze each almond between your fingers. The white nut will pop out of the brown skin. Discard the skins.

Place nuts in single layer on cookie sheet. Pat with a damp hand to moisten the nuts. Sprinkle lightly with salt. Put into a very slow oven (250 degrees). Stir once in a while. The nuts are ready to eat when they're dry enough to snap in half. Use potholder to remove cookie sheet from oven and place on cooling rack. Store in covered container when completely cooled.

☆ SOLAR WALNUTS

walnuts	*sieve or wire basket*
water	*saucepan with lid*
	bowl
	cookie sheet
	potholders or mitts
	wire rack
	mixing spoon

Fill saucepan half full of water, cover with lid, place over medium heat, and bring to a boil. Put shelled walnut kernels in a sieve and lower into pan. (Younger astrocooks should ask an adult to help in taking nuts in and out of boiling water.) Let nuts boil for 3 minutes. Lift out sieve and nuts and set over a bowl to drain. Shake from time to time. Heat oven to 350 degrees.

Spread walnuts in an even layer on cookie sheet and place in hot oven. Bake for 12 to 15 minutes, stirring often. When kernels are toasted golden brown, use potholders or mitts to remove tray to cooling rack.

☆ SUNFLOWER SEEDS

sunflower head

strainer
cookie sheet
mixing spoon
wire rack
potholders or mitts

Remove seeds from sunflower when ripe: the flower head will be drooping and the seeds will be hard and black-striped. Pick out the seeds, put them in a strainer, and rinse in cold water. Pour seeds in a single layer on a cookie sheet. Place in 250 degree oven and stir occasionally. It takes about 2 hours for seeds to dry. Use potholders or mitts to move tray to cooling rack.

Astroriddles: Why is the letter *F* like a rocket failure? *Because it makes "all" "fall."*

What letter in the alphabet can travel the greatest distance? *The letter* E. *It goes to the end of space and the end of time.*

Why is the letter *A* like a colony garden in full bloom? *Because a* B *(bee) is always after it.*

What letter will set a heavenly body moving? *The letter* T. *It will make a "star" "start."*

☆ SURVIVAL MIX I

If you ever find yourself stranded on a deserted planet, let's hope your spacesuit pockets are stuffed with one of the following recipes.

1 cup raisins	*paring knife*
1 cup of any other kind of dried fruit (apple, banana, apricot, etc.)	*cutting board*
	container with tight lid
1 cup peanuts, walnuts, almonds, or mixed nuts	
1 cup shelled sunflower seeds	

Using paring knife and cutting board, chop dried fruit and nuts into pieces. Put pieces into container with raisins and sunflower seeds, fasten the lid, and shake to mix well. This mix is especially good with a frosty glass of milk. *Makes 4 cups.*

☆ SURVIVAL MIX II

1 cup dried bananas	*paring knife*
1 cup raisins	*cutting board*
1 cup unsweetened coconut flakes	*container with tight lid*
3 cups mixed nuts	

Using paring knife and cutting board, chop dried banana into pieces. Place raisins, coconut flakes, and nuts in container. Add banana pieces, fasten the lid, and shake to mix well. *Makes 6 cups.*

☆ SURVIVAL MIX III

Put the following into a very large bowl:

14 cups (1 big box)	*very large bowl*
old-fashioned oatmeal	*measuring cup*
2 cups wheat germ	*measuring spoons*
2 cups raisins	*small bowl*
1 cup shelled sunflower	*shallow pans*
seeds	*long-handled spatula*
1 cup sesame seeds	*potholders or mitts*
2 cups chopped walnuts	*cooling racks*
1 cup brown sugar	

Sprinkle with salt.
Combine the following ingredients in small bowl and mix well.

1 cup water
1 cup corn oil
½ tsp vanilla
3 tbsp honey

Dribble the second mixture over the dry ingredients in the large bowl. (Be sure your hands and fingernails are clean.) Then use your hands to mix all the ingredients together until everything feels moistened. Pour into shallow pans, smooth into an even layer, and bake in a very slow oven (200 degrees) for 3 hours. Use a spatula to turn and mix the ingredients every 30 minutes. Use potholders or mitts to move the trays to cooling racks. When cool, store in containers with tight lids. *Makes 5 quarts.*

Astrotip: For hikes or school lunches, place ½ cup servings of any Survival Mix into plastic sandwich bags. Fasten with wire twistees.

Astrojoke:
Space passenger on Neptune: "Oh, Robot. I'm ready to leave. Would you call me a starship, please?"
Robot: "Certainly, sir. You're a starship."

Astrofact: Neptune is the eighth planet from our sun, but sometimes Pluto's unusual orbit brings it inside Neptune's orbit for several years. When that happens, Pluto could be called the eighth planet.

Astroriddle: What has four legs and no head and wags its tail? *A space dog with its head in a bowl of Star Shower Popcorn.*

☆☆ STAR SHOWER POPCORN

When you serve this snack to your crew—watch out! It disappears faster than the shower from a shooting star.

Cheddar and Monterey Jack cheese	*paring knife*
½ cup unpopped popcorn	*cutting board*
2 tbsp vegetable oil	*large covered saucepan*
¼ cup butter or margarine	*or skillet*
	potholder or mitt
	large serving bowl or
	4 small bowls

On the cutting board, cut a slice about ¼ inch thick from the end of a chunk of Monterey Jack cheese. Cut another slice from the end of a chunk of Cheddar cheese. (Or use all Monterey Jack cheese, or all Cheddar cheese.) Cut each slice in half lengthwise, then cut across the slices to make tiny cubes and set aside.

Pour about 2 tablespoons oil into saucepan or skillet. (There should be enough to lightly cover the bottom of the pan.) Place pan over medium heat for a minute or two, then add about ½ cup popcorn, or just enough to cover the bottom of the pan.

Place lid on pan and stand by until you hear the first kernel pop. Then, using potholder or mitt, shake the pan gently while the rest of the corn is popping. At first the kernels will pop very quickly. Gradually the popping will slow down. When the kernels seem to be popping very slowly, it's time to turn off the heat. But leave the pan on the burner with the lid on for a few more minutes while the last kernels pop. Now pour popcorn into the large bowl or into four small bowls. In the same saucepan or skillet, melt about ¼ cup (½ stick) of butter or margarine over *low* heat. Slowly pour the melted butter or margarine over the popcorn and stir to mix well. (Or ask a crew member to stir the popcorn while you slowly pour the melted butter or margarine.) Sprinkle popcorn lightly with salt and stir again. Top with tiny cheese chunks. (Don't stir after adding cheese or it will all end up on the bottom.)

Serve with paper napkins and cold crunchy apples or tall glasses of chilled fruit juice for a very special snack. *Serves 4.*

Astrotip: For the crispiest popcorn ever, keep unpopped kernels stored in a covered jar in the refrigerator.

Astroriddle: What should you offer a space monster who stops in for snacks? *Anything it wants.*

☆ SUNFLAKES

Melted cheese and chopped herbs on hot potato chips for a solar special!

2 cups potato chips
Cheddar cheese

1 tbsp dried herbs: choose from marjoram or basil or thyme

shallow pan
grater
small bowl
measuring cup
measuring spoons
potholder or mitts
wire rack

Heat oven to 350 degrees. Grate cheese into bowl to measure ½ cup and set aside. Shake potato chips onto shallow

154

pan and spread with your clean hands to make a single layer. Use your fingers to sprinkle the cheese across the top of the potato chips. Take a few dried herbs at a time between your fingers and crumble them over the chips and cheese. Put the tray in the oven for 5 minutes or until the cheese melts. Use potholders or mitts to move the tray to the cooling rack. Serve the chips while cheese is still melty-hot. Or serve them when they've cooled. They're good both ways. *Serves 4.*

Astrofact: Neptune may have a solid core, but this planet is covered with thick clouds of methane and other gasses. Nine or ten narrow rings circle Neptune, with huge gaps between them. They reflect little or no light. One theory is that the rings may be gassy trails left by satellites circling the planet.

NEPTUNE PUZZLE

Across:

2. Neptune is thought to be a gaseous giant like Saturn and _____.

4. Uranus, Neptune, and Pluto are called the _____ planets.

7. Counting from the sun, what number planet is Neptune?

9. Saturn and Neptune both have these.

11. What gas gives Neptune its color?

12. Neptune is covered with thick _____.

Down:

1. Neptune is how many times larger than Earth? (two words)

3. Neptune may have a solid _____.

5. What planet sometimes moves inside Neptune's orbit?

6. The rings around Neptune may be gassy _____ behind satellites.

8. Neptune's color.

10. The rings are so narrow, there is more _____ than ring.

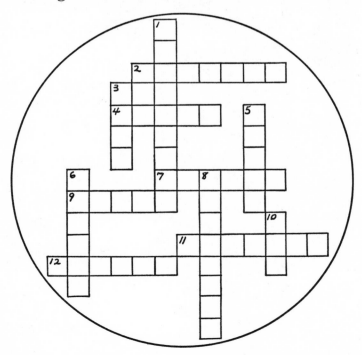

PLUTO PARTY PLANS AND PUNCHES

Happy Birthday, Dear Taryo

Greidey threw down his shovel. "We're never going to find anything in this dumb old mine." He jammed his hands into the pockets of his ice-suit. "So why should I stay and work while you go home?"

"It will only be for an hour," Father said, "and Taryo will still be helping. But I must go bake the Battlestar Bread for his party."

"I'm the oldest," Greidey whined. "The first party on Pluto should be mine."

"But it's Taryo's birthday," Father answered, "and we want to surprise him. You two keep working here and come back to the village in an hour."

Greidey grumbled and grabbed his shovel. He tossed a scoop of dirt on the conveyor and watched as his father hurried toward the frosty village.

At the other end of the conveyor, Greidey knew Taryo

would be waiting to search the screens for any sign of gold or gems or anything the villagers felt would make it worthwhile to colonize this planet.

"Taryo gets the easy job. He gets the party. He has all the friends. And Father likes him best. But maybe . . ." Greidey dropped his shovel again. "Maybe I can change all that."

He raced away to the screening shack. "Taryo!" he called. "Guess what! Father said we could take the rest of the day off. Let's go play!"

Taryo peered through the doorway. "You sure it's okay?"

"Sure! Come on, I know a new game." Quickly he led Taryo to the center of the ice forest. Here, one tree looked exactly like the next one.

"We're going to play Hide and Hunt," said Greidey. "Close your eyes and count to 100. Then take 300 steps toward those faraway glacier mountains before you come looking for me. I'll be hiding anywhere except in the village. Got it?"

Taryo nodded and closed his eyes.

Greidey hurried home. He told his father, "Taryo ran off to play as soon as you left. But I told him he's supposed to be home in an hour."

As the guests arrived and asked for Taryo, Greidey said, "He'll be here in a minute. Wanna play Tilt-a-Planet with me?"

"We'll wait for Taryo."

"Have some Battlestar Bread then."

"We'd rather wait for our friend."

"Well, let's play Feed-the-Space-Spider while we wait."

The guests shook their heads.

"I'm getting worried," Father said finally. "I'd better go look for Taryo."

"We'll come with you!" cried the guests.

"Go on, then," Greidey grumbled. "See if I care." All by

himself, he gobbled six Pluto Party Pops and half the Battlestar Bread. Then he lay down on the couch with his hands on his aching stomach until he heard shouting and laughter outside.

"Hurray for Taryo! Taryo's our hero!"

Father burst into the house, carrying Taryo on his shoulder. The party guests followed closely behind. Their ice-suits clinked and clattered with every step.

"That was the worst trick you've ever pulled." Father frowned at Greidey, then he grinned and swung Taryo down to the floor. "But thanks to your brother, it worked out just fine. When he got tired of hunting for you, he went back to your job at the mine. And look what he found!"

The guests emptied their pockets, laughing and piling the table high with glittering, gleaming ice-opals.

"Now we'll be able to stay and build a new colony on this planet," said Father, "and we'll name the colony . . ."

"TARYOPAL!" shouted the guests.

Greidey turned his face away and clutched his stomach and groaned.

Astrofact: Pluto, a small cold planet, has no satellite. This planet is far, far away (3,664 million miles) from the sun. From Pluto the sun looks like just another distant light in the sky. On Pluto years are longer than on any other known planet—it takes about 250 Earth years for Pluto to make one orbit around the sun. Cethane ice, water ice, and ammonia ice are believed to cover the planet's surface.

If you would like to plan an interplanetary party—a Mars party, Saturn party, Star Trader, or Star Watch party, or some other celebration—we have the plans for you.

ASTRO-INVITATIONS

Cut large circles from construction paper. Use a felt-tip pen or crayon to copy these invitations onto each circle. (Of course, you'll put your own name, date, and address on the ones you make.) Here are three suggestions:

Now, slip the invitation into an envelope *or* take one long rocket-shaped balloon for each guest. Use a dark felt-tip pen to write SURPRISE INSIDE on each of the balloons. Then roll each invitation so it forms a small tube, slip one into each balloon, blow up the balloons, tie them closed, and deliver to your friends. *Or* don't blow air into the balloons—just poke in the rolled invitation, slip the balloons into envelopes, and mail to your friends.

Astroriddle: Why did the astrocook bring a fig to the Star
Watch party? *He couldn't get a date.*

Here's another way to make your invitations. Using construction paper, cut out a rocket about nine inches long.
Draw the rocket design, add the party information, and
color it. Make one for each guest you wish to invite. Fold the
rockets, put them in envelopes, and deliver them or mail
them to your friends. *Or* cut the rockets into jigsaw-puzzle
pieces and put the pieces into envelopes. When you friends
put the pieces together, they'll be able to read your invitation.

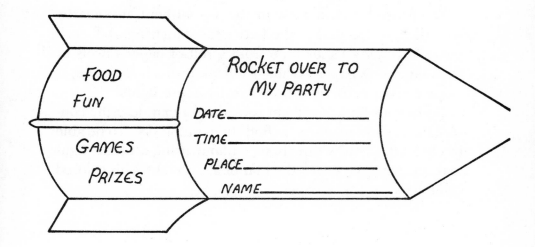

Astroriddle: How does a three-headed Saturnian sand-slipper count his thirteen party guests? *On thirteen of his fingers.*

Use space themes for any kind of party *or* plan a special party.

STAR TRADER LUNCH PARTY

Plan a picnic. Ask each astroguest to bring his own secret lunch in a decorated box or bag. Collect all the lunches in one place. When it's time to eat, play a game such as Feed The Space Spiders. Guest with the highest score has first choice of lunches. (No fair peeking inside before choosing.) Second highest score gets second choice, and so on.

Astrofact: Information from the Apollo Moon Landings tells us that the dark features that make up the face of the "man-in-the-moon" are really basalt-covered basins left from ancient lava flows.

STAR WATCH PARTY

Nine o'clock in the evening is a good time for a Star Watch Party. If you're having friends sleep over, or having a slumber party, here are some party plans.

You'll need a clear view of the sky without any nearby streetlights—the darker the better for stargazing. Ask each guest to bring a paper tube from a roll of paper towels or from wrapping paper. When you look through the tube, it helps cut out extra light from nearby house lights.

Go to your library and get some books that describe constellations and tell where to find them in the sky. To be able to check the book's directions without using a bright light make a star light: cover the end of a flashlight with colored cellophane or tissue paper.

Astroexperiment: The skies seem to move as the Earth turns. You can prove the turning of the Earth for yourself. Find a clear view of the sky, with a corner of a house or other building to your right. Lie down or sit in a chair with your head back so that you are perfectly still. Now choose some stars close to the edge of the house. You'll see them gradually move closer and closer to the house until they disappear from your view.

Astrofact: There are half a million galaxies in the bowl of the Big Dipper constellation.

ASTROCONTESTS

To make your party more exciting, you may want to stage several contests to see who will be the first to find certain constellations, who can find the Big Dipper without help, the Little Dipper, the Milky Way. Perhaps your astroguests will recognize other constellations. Orion is easy to recognize—three bright stars in a row form Orion's belt; three faint stars hang below the belt, like a sword in a jeweled scabbard. The middle one is not a star at all but a huge mass of glowing gas called the Orion Nebula. Cassiopeia is easy to recognize, too. It looks like a stretched out W. See how many more constellations you can find.

PLANETS

You can see five planets without a telescope. You can tell by the steadiness of its light if it's a planet. The stars appear to twinkle.

Jupiter is bright white in the southeast during autumn, and in the southwest during winter. If you have binoculars, you may be able to locate Jupiter's four brightest moons near the planet.

Saturn looks bright yellow-white. Look southeast in the

spring, southwest in the summer to see this planet. You can't see the rings of Saturn with binoculars—you would need a telescope to see them.

Mars is a reddish color. It's closer to the sun than the other planets, so its orbit is shorter, letting it move more quickly across the sky. Check a book on astronomy for instructions on where to look for Mars around the time you're planning your party.

Venus is a bright white—brighter than the other planets. Like Mars, Venus changes locations in the sky very quickly. Use your book on astronomy to locate Venus around the time of your party.

Mercury is so close to the sun it is hard to find. You should never look directly at the sun, but just past sunset during March and April, Mercury can be located in the sky.

Astrofact: Triton, one of Neptune's moons, is larger than Earth's moon. Scientists believe Triton may crash into Neptune within the next 100 years.

STAR SHOWERS

Celestial fireworks shine in our sky when meteor swarms come into our atmosphere and burn. Several times a year the Earth passes through known meteor showers (particles left by comets, moving on parallel paths around the sun).

The best way to watch for meteors is to lie flat on your back on the ground and search the sky. Look in the direction of the constellations listed below on the dates given, especially for the Perseids, the "Old Faithful" of meteor swarms.

Name of Meteor Swarm	Constellation Where Seen	Date Expected
Lyrids	Vega—Hercules	April 20-22
Aquarids	Aquarius—look toward great square of Pegasus	May 4-6

164

Perseids	Perseus	August 10-13
Orionids	Gemini—Orion	October 18-23
Taurids	Auriga—Taurus	October 31-November 6
Geminids	Castor in Gemini	December 9-13

Astrojoke: Overheard at a space colony party:

First Astronaut: "I believe that Martian shrimp I just swallowed was still alive!"

Second Astronaut: "Should you take something for it?"

First Astronaut: "No, I'll let it starve."

STAR WATCH PARTY FOOD SUGGESTIONS

Star Shower Popcorn (Chapter 10)
 or Survival Mix (Chapter 10)
Apples
Punch (See below)
Inner Space Cookies (Chapter 9)
   or
Solar Debris (Chapter 10)
Bananas
Punch (See below)
Cosmic Cookies (Chapter 9)
   or
Carrot and Celery Strips
Day-side Dip and Chips (Chapter 3)
Punch (See below)
Cave Rocks (Chapter 9)

Astroriddle: Is it better to stir Dark-side Punch on a full stomach or an empty stomach? *It's better to stir it on the stove.*

☆ ORANGE GALAXY PUNCH

We live in the Milky Way Galaxy. Do you suppose there is an Orange Galaxy somewhere in the universe?

2 cups orange juice
2 tbsp honey
4 large marshmallows

measuring cup and spoons
small saucepan
potholder or mitt
mixing spoon
serving cups

Pour orange juice into saucepan. Add honey and stir while heating. (Do not boil.) When hot, place a large marshmallow into each serving cup and fill cup with punch. *Serves 4.*

☆ DARK-SIDE PUNCH

The dark side is the part of a planet which has turned away from its sun. Dark-side Punch is good to warm you up when your planet has turned away from the sun.

3 cups grape juice
9 whole cloves

measuring cup
small saucepan
serving cups

Pour grape juice into saucepan. Add cloves. Heat just until steaming. Do not boil. Pour into cups. *Serves 4.*

Astroknock Knock: Who's there? Comet. Comet who? Don't comet (comment) if you don't like the punch.

☆ STAR BUBBLE BEVERAGE

Punch with a twinkle.

1 12-oz can ginger ale	*2 quart pitcher or*
1 quart orange juice	*punch bowl*
1 12-oz can pineapple	*can opener*
juice	*mixing spoon*

Chill all ingredients. Just before serving combine all three in pitcher or punch bowl. Serve over orange Neptune Slurpies (Chapter 10) instead of ice cubes. *Serves 6 to 8.*

Astrofact: You can begin to understand the distance to Pluto when you know that it takes five hours for light from the sun to reach that planet. It takes only three minutes for sunlight to reach planet Mercury.

ASTRODECORATIONS

Front Door: Tie round balloons on strings (these are the planets) and hang them over the top of the door so the planets are on the outside, the strings on the inside. Tie the string ends to the inside doorknob. Write the names of the planets on the balloons, using a felt-tip pen. If you have a choice of colors, use an orange or red balloon for Mars, yellow balloons for Saturn and Jupiter, a blue one for Earth, green balloons for Uranus and Neptune, and white for Venus, Mercury, and Pluto.

For a Mars party, use all red balloons. For a Saturn party, use all yellow. For an Earth party, use all blue.

Party Room: Pick out nine more balloons to represent all the planets. Fasten them over the party table with static electricity—just rub each inflated balloon several times across the back of your arm or on top of your head, then

167

push the balloon against the ceiling. It will stick. Put up a larger balloon to represent the sun.

Hang crepe paper streamers across the room to represent the Milky Way. If you wish, put lots of stick-on foil stars on the streamers.

Tablecloth: Stick colored foil stars on tablecloth, or cut star shapes and planet shapes from construction paper and place them over the tablecloth. If it's a birthday party, make one big cardboard star and cover it with silver foil. Use it as a place mat for the birthday crew member.

Or for special parties, use the ideas above in different ways. For a Mars party, decorate with red balloons and streamers and use a red crepe-paper tablecloth. Make a punch of Cran-apple juice and ginger ale, and serve red apples and Creamy Planets (made from strawberry ice cream) along with your other refreshments.

For a Saturn party, decorate with yellow balloons, streamers, and tablecloth. Serve Star Bubble Beverage, bananas, and Creamy Planets (made with pineapple sherbet) with your other refreshments.

Astrofact: The planet Pluto has an unusual orbital path which makes some scientists believe it was once a moon of Neptune.

ASTROPRIZES AND FAVORS

Select prizes and favors with the space theme in mind. Look for miniature space toys, space-type jigsaw puzzles, space comics or coloring books, writing pads and notebooks with space pictures for covers. Small covered puzzle games that have tiny balls that must be manipulated into holes are fun (and great to carry aboard a spaceship—no loose parts). Any gadget with a space theme makes a great party favor; for example, pencil sharpeners shaped like rockets.

168

Astrofact: Pluto, the farthest planet from our sun, was discovered in 1930. But it isn't always the farthest away. Soon, Pluto's unusual orbit will swing it closer to the sun than its neighbor Neptune. (Pluto takes about 250 years to orbit the sun.) For twenty years, it will be the eighth planet, traveling inside Neptune's orbit, so that Neptune will be ninth in distance from the sun.

ASTROPARTY DATES

You may plan a party anytime—for birthdays, to welcome new neighbors or classmates, to celebrate the first or last day of vacation, or the Fourth of July, or *any* holiday, or just because you feel like a party. Or you may want to celebrate special dates in the exploration of space. Here are some space dates for party-planning.

July 20 . . . on this date in 1969 the lunar module Eagle landed on the moon's Sea of Tranquility. Astronaut Neil Armstrong took humanity's first step on the moon.

February 20 . . . on this date in 1962 astronaut John Glenn made the first manned orbital flight for the United States, circling Earth three times.

April 12 . . . on this date in 1961 Russian cosmonaut Yuri Gagarin became the first human in space, orbiting Earth one time.

May 5 . . . on this date in 1961 Alan Shepard became the first U. S. astronaut to leave Earth's surface—a suborbital flight to an altitude of 115 miles.

July 20 . . . on this date in 1976 the U. S. Viking I lander set down on Mars to send back photos and information.

August 12 . . . on this date in 1977 the NASA space shuttle Enterprise made its first practice flight, landing in the Mojave Desert.

Astroriddle: What time is it when you divide Battlestar Bread among four hungry astronauts? *A quarter to four.*

ASTROPARTY FOOD

Battlestar Bread, Chapter 5, makes a great change from party cake. Make it with honey, zucchini, nuts, and raisins and bake it in a bowl. For special parties, fortunetelling favors can be twisted into waxed paper and stirred into the batter before baking. Guests read their future from the chart below:

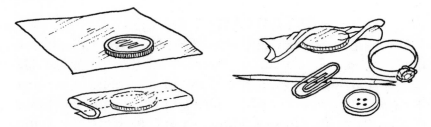

BATTLESTAR BREAD ASTROFUTURES

Paper clip: you will work with space research.
Button: you will design sizzling space fashions.
Dime: you will find an asteroid silver mine.
Ring: you will live on a wheel colony.
Penny: you will be a poor, but happy, asteroid miner.
Toothpick: you will be a famous astrocook.
(Try to think of more favors and Astrofutures to bake in the bread.)

Astroriddle: When does an Astrocrew eat? *At launch time.*

PARTY FOOD SUGGESTIONS

Creamy Planets: Chapter 9
Starshine Ice Cream: Chapter 9
Orange Galaxy Punch: Chapter 11
Dark-Side Punch: Chapter 11
Star Bubble Beverage: Chapter 11
Pluto Party Pops: Chapter 9
Neptune Slurpies: Chapter 10

Star Shower Popcorn: Chapter 10
Super Green Spaceship Supreme: Chapter 9
Sat-On Sandwiches: Chapter 8
Leader Sandwiches: Chapter 8
Cosmic or Inner Space Cookies: Chapter 9
Cave Rocks: Chapter 9
Sunflakes: Chapter 10
Mercury Dips: Chapter 3
Planetray: Chapter 3
Cheese Meteors: Chapter 3
Star Melts: Chapter 7
Marshmallow Robots: Chapter 9

Astrotwister: Say this five times fast: Pluto's plentiful playful pals.

GALACTIC GAMES

These pencil-and-paper games can start a party while you're waiting for the rest of the guests to arrive. Or use them to settle your guests again after several active games. (You'll find active games later in this chapter.)

SCRAMBLE A PLANET

Before the party, prepare a paper for each guest with the names of the planets scrambled as follows:

1. preijtu
2. sarm
3. snuve
4. crrumey
5. retah
6. narusu
7. otulp
8. punteen
9. nutsra

Give each player one of the prepared papers, a pencil, and a magazine to support the paper. The first to unscramble all the planet names is the winner. Have another prize ready for the first to put all the unscrambled names in the correct order in which they orbit the sun.

Unscrambled Names	Orbiting Order
1. Jupiter	1. Mercury
2. Mars	2. Venus
3. Venus	3. Earth
4. Mercury	4. Mars
5. Earth	5. Jupiter
6. Uranus	6. Saturn
7. Pluto	7. Uranus
8. Neptune	8. Neptune
9. Saturn	9. Pluto

ASTROSTORY

Have your guests sit in a circle. Give each player a piece of paper, a pencil, and a magazine to support the paper while writing. Now, read aloud the beginning lines of the following story:

The daring young astronauts, Trylla and Jack, ran into a bit of trouble the last time they went exploring. They were about to land on a planet where no humans had ever been before when suddenly . . .

The first player then writes "Number 1" on his paper, finishes the story sentence, and writes three more sentences that continue to tell the story. He reads aloud *only* his last sentence. The next player writes "Number 2" on his paper, then writes three more sentences to continue the story. He reads aloud *only* the last sentence. Then the third player writes his share of the story, and continue around the circle, with each player numbering his paper and writing three sentences about the story. Remember to read aloud *only* the last sentence each time. The last player in the circle writes three sentences to end the story.

Now, gather all the papers in order and read aloud the strange story from beginning to end.

STAR RIDDLES

Here are some riddles to stump your guests.

What star is a problem to a colony housekeeper? *Stardust.*

What star is not very bright? Stardom *(star dumb).*

What star do you catch from seas of space? *Starfish.*

What star is the right-hand side of the spaceship? *Starboard.*

What star do Earth explorers put on a new planet? *Star-Spangled Banner.*

ASTROTEST

See how many words your guests can make from the letters spelling **astrocook.**

Astroriddle: Twelve-year-old Harold had two Pluto Pops when the ship stopped at Vega IV. The brother of the ship's captain had three pops, but the man who had the three pops doesn't have a brother. How can this be? *The captain was a woman.*

MORE ACTIVE GALACTIC GAMES

Have prizes ready, but don't be surprised if your guests ask to play these games over and over "just for fun."

ASTEROID MINERS

Give each guest a rocket-shaped (long) balloon. Put a cardboard circle on the floor or ground for a launching pad. Put other cardboard markers around the area at varying distances from the launching pad—these are asteroids. Each miner takes a turn standing on the pad, blowing up a balloon, then releasing it into space. Give points to the miner whose rocket comes closest to touching or landing on an asteroid.

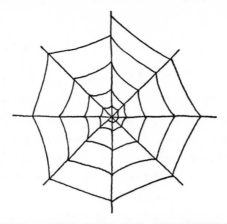

FEED THE SPACE SPIDERS

One of the earlier space experiments sent spiders into orbit. For this game, astroguests take turns feeding the spiders. Draw a web-shaped pattern on a large cardboard, or scratch it into the dirt if you're outdoors. Mark point values in each web section, ten points for small areas, one point for large ones. Give each astroguest five colored markers (or beans, pennies, buttons, etc.). Take turns tossing the markers to the web to "feed the spiders." Player with the highest score wins.

PLUTO KICK

Astroguests form relay teams. First player in each team is given a round balloon, representing the planet Pluto. Place a cardboard circle several feet ahead of each team. These represent the planet Neptune. Team members take turns kicking the planet Pluto (no hands) to and around Neptune and back to the next player in line. First team with all members to orbit Neptune and return wins the game. (If too hard a kick causes Pluto to Nova—explode—that team automatically forfeits the game!)

FLYING SAUCERS

Set a basket on a table indoors or outdoors and cover it with foil if you like. Give each guest three chances to hurl a paper plate (flying saucer) into the basket from a marked launching pad line.

ROCKET LAUNCH

This is an outdoor game. You'll need an empty tube, like the ones inside wrapping paper or paper kitchen towels—the longer the better. Set nine targets at varying distances from a marked launching pad. The targets represent the nine planets. They can be empty boxes, baskets, plastic bowls, etc. Give each a different point value (write this on a slip of paper and put it inside each container).

In the solar system, Jupiter and Saturn are the largest, Uranus and Neptune are next largest, then Earth and Venus, then Mars. Mercury and Pluto are the smallest. Keep this in mind when planning your targets.

Now, ask each astroguest to take a turn standing on the launching pad and sending ships to the planets. To do this, drop marbles into the tube, one at a time. Hold the tube at waist level, then launch the marble into space toward any of the planets. Each guest gets three tries. Highest score wins.

ALIEN INVADERS

You'll need a bag of unshelled peanuts to be the alien invaders. Tie colored yarns around some of them—one color for commanders, another color for warriors, a third color for officers, and the plain peanuts (most of them) are the alien ships' crews. Give point values to the different colors, highest for commanders, and so on. Hide the peanuts around the party room, or around the lawn, Give guests paper bags and order them to find and collect the alien invaders. Give prizes to the astroguest who collects the most and to the astroguest who has the highest number of points.

Astrofact: In Earth's gravity, if you throw a ball into the air, it will fall back to the ground. In zero gravity, if you throw a ball into the air, it will keep on moving away.

ASTEROID TOSS

You'll need a large cardboard carton. Turn it upside down so the open side is on the floor. Using a felt-tip pen, write ASTEROID TOSS across the top or on a side of the carton which has no printing. Now draw four asteroids. (The size depends on whether you will be tossing beanbags, jar lids, or marbles through the cutout asteroids. If you use jar lids, the lids should be the same size and as small as possible. But draw the·asteroids different sizes.)

For Marbles: Draw one asteroid 2 inches across, two asteroids 3 inches across, and a large asteroid 4 inches across.

For Jar Lids (no wider than 2½ inches): Draw one asteroid 3½ inches across, two asteroids 4½ inches across, and one asteroid 5½ inches across.

For Beanbags (no larger than 3 inches): Draw one asteroid 4 inches across, two 5 inches, and one 6 inches.

Use a craft knife or paring knife to cut out each asteroid. (Younger party planners should ask an adult to help.) Label the largest asteroid "Ceres − 5 points." Label the next two "Pallas + 5 points" and "Juno + 5 points." Label the smallest asteroid "Vesta + 10 points."

Each player has four tosses. High score wins. Remember, score 10 points for a toss through Vesta, 5 points for Pallas or Juno, but take 5 points *off* the score for a toss through big Ceres.

Astrofact: Zero gravity doesn't really mean no gravity. There is no place known in the universe that actually has no gravity. So zero gravity really means low gravity.

TILT A PLANET

You'll need a cardboard lid from a large shoe box or gift box. On the cardboard, draw the sun and planets as shown below, remembering that Mercury is smallest, Jupiter largest, Earth and Venus about the same size. Even Mercury must be large enough for a marble to roll through it. Now cut out the sun and planets using a craft knife or paring knife. (Younger party planners should ask an adult for help.) Label each planet. Pluto counts +10, Jupiter and the sun both count −5. Saturn counts −1. The others have no score. Somewhere on the board, write the words TILT A PLANET. On the left side of the sun draw a small circle and label it "start."

For large groups make two boards exactly alike and divide your guests into two teams.

As a special surprise, make enough boards so each of your friends can have one to take home.

To play, hold the board in both hands, with your left thumb beside (but not touching) Mars, and your right thumb beside (but not touching) Earth. Another player places a marble on the circle marked "start." Tilt the board and try to roll the marble to the far end and through the hole marked "Pluto." Try to keep the marble from rolling through any of the other openings.

Each player is allowed one practice turn. Then each player rolls three marbles one at a time, while the other guests watch and total the score. Highest score wins.

Astroquestion: Are there more than nine planets orbiting our sun? Perhaps you will be the one to discover a planet no one has seen before. What will you name it?

177

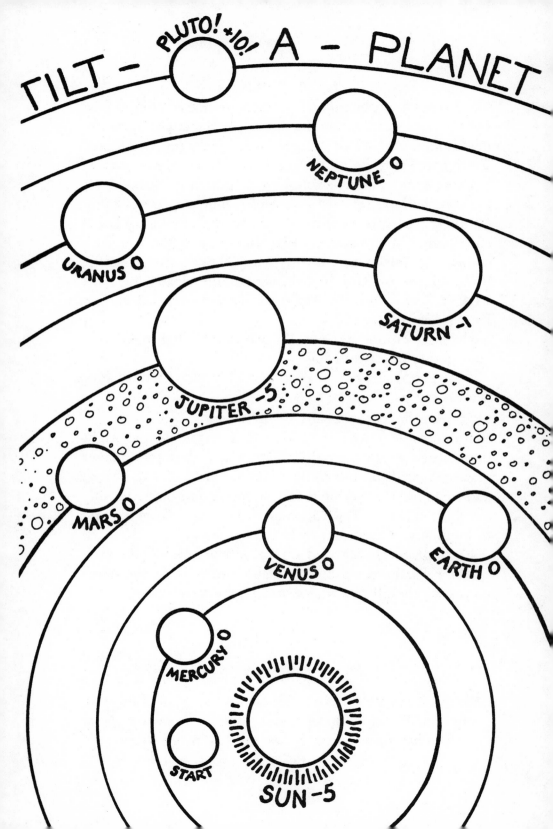

PLUTO PUZZLE

Across:

3. There are half a million _____ in the bowl of the Big Dipper constellation.
5. _____ is one of Neptune's moons.
7. Pluto may once have been a moon of _____.

Down:

1. _____ is a cold planet.
2. Light from our sun reaches the planet Mercury in three _____.
3. Zero gravity really means low _____.
4. How many hours does it take for light from our sun to reach the planet Pluto?
6. How many times will Pluto orbit the sun in 300 years?

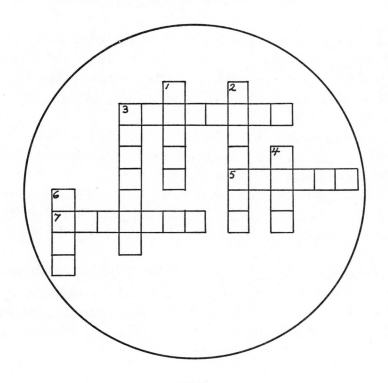

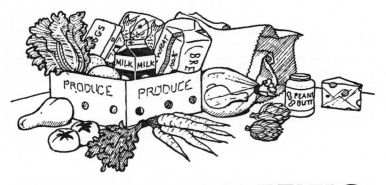

MILKWAY MENUS
For Balanced Meals

Berryhill Boredom

Ellen was excited that her mother and father were to be the very first Earth ambassadors to the newly discovered planet called Berryhill. But when they reached the planet, her parents said Ellen would have to stay in the embassy during the visit.

"We know very little about the Berryhill natives," her mother explained. "We can't take any chances that we might offend or insult them by accident."

"You might say or do something wrong without meaning to," her father added. "It's much safer for you and for the Earth mission here if you stay in the embassy during our visit."

It was boring to stay in the embassy. There was nothing to do but listen to storytapes and stare out the window. The planet looked very much like Earth. Ellen couldn't see any of the natives, but she could see why the first spacemen to find the planet called it Berryhill. Blackberry-type brambles grew in profusion just outside the embassy wall.

The more Ellen looked at the blackberry bushes, the more bored she became with staying at the embassy. Besides, she was hungry. She didn't like strange alien food. The blackberries didn't look alien.

One of the bushes was close to the window. Ellen looked hard at the ripe berries growing on the bush. They looked just like blackberries at home.

"I could slip out without anyone seeing me and pick some berries," Ellen said to herself. "I know I could do it without being seen. I can't insult the natives if I don't even see them. Mother and Father would be happy to have blackberries for dessert. And it would give me something to do."

She found a bowl in the embassy kitchen, then carefully opened the back door. There was no one around.

Ellen stayed close to the wall as she tiptoed to the corner, then along the wall by her window. There was the bush. The berries looked better than ever.

She listened and looked as hard as she could. No, there was no sound. There was no movement. She was alone. Ellen hurried to the bush and picked until the bowl was full and her fingers were stained purple.

She was safely back inside the embassy kitchen with the berries in a bowl beside her, glancing through recipe tapes, when her mother came in.

"Ellen," her mother said, frowning. "Perhaps you had better come in here. I don't understand it, but one of the Berryhill plant men is at the door. He says you have all his children."

Astroriddle: Can an astrocook on the moon jump higher than his stove? *Of course he can. The stove can't jump.*

Astrofact: Our solar system is just one tiny part of the whirling pinwheel galaxy known as the Milky Way. A galaxy is a system of stars, or a stellar universe. The Milky Way galaxy looks like a giant spinning pinwheel, with our solar system on one arm of the wheel.

Astrotip: On the faraway story-planet of Braxtl (see Chapter 7), only one food can be grown. This claylike bread which the natives eat provides all the vitamins, proteins, and minerals needed to keep their bodies in tiptop condition. The natives only need to eat three loaves of Braxtl bread daily to keep their bodies healthy, their skin bright and blue, their hair green and glossy. *There is only one problem.* On Braxtl, eating is a bore.

Earthlings are luckier. Their planet produces a tremendous variety of nutritious, delicious, interesting foods. Good things to eat on this planet come in all sizes, shapes, colors, textures, and flavors. There are so many different ones that scientists have found it necessary to classify them into four different groups. *There is only one problem.* On Earth, everyone who wants to keep in tiptop condition must remember to eat some foods from each of these four groups every day. But that isn't hard to do. And fortunately on Earth, *eating never needs to be a bore!*

Here's how it works. Think of the four food groups as four parts of a rocket:

Milk Group

Have at least three servings daily of milk, buttermilk, cottage cheese or other natural cheese.

Nose Cone

Grain Group

Eat three or four servings daily of whole grain breads and cereals (unsugared), rice, macaroni, noodles, or spaghetti.

Instrument Panel

Fruit and Vegetable Group

Eat four or more servings daily—include one dark green and one yellow vegetable and one citrus fruit or tomato each day.

Booster

Protein Group

Eat two servings daily of fish, poultry, eggs, natural cheese, meat, dried beans, dried peas, nuts, or peanut butter.

Fuel System

Just as you need all four components to build an efficient rocket, you need all four food groups to build a healthy—and efficient—body.

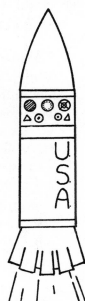

Just for fun, you might think of it this way:

An Earthling who drank 13 gallons of milk and ate 1 grape daily would be like a rocket with a huge nosecone, a tiny booster, no instrument panel, and no fuel system.

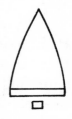

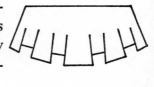

An Earthling who ate 27 loaves of bread and 1 egg every day would be like a rocket with a huge instrument panel, part of a fuel system, and nothing else.

An Earthling who ate 6 heads of cabbage, 94 carrots, 2 green beans and a bunch of bananas every day would be like a rocket with no nose cone, no instruments, and no fuel system. All by itself, the booster wouldn't get very far into space.

And of course an Earthing who ate 4 hamburger patties, 3 T-bone steaks, 1¾ pounds of cheese, and a slice of bacon each day would be all fuel system with nothing to propel and no way to navigate.

Worse yet, an Earthling who ate only candy morning, noon, and night would be like nothing at all—nothing but empty candy wrappers.

Astrotip: Consider the seasons when planning your menus. Foods are most economical when they are in season. And the foods you enjoy on a cold wintry night might not be as enjoyable on a sunny summer afternoon. Following are some menu ideas to help you get started planning well balanced meals:

SPRING MENUS

Breakfast
   fresh strawberries or fruit juice
   Sizzling Stars, Chapter 2
   milk

Lunch
   Black Holes, Chapter 3
   Galactic Choice Sandwiches, Chapter 8
   Survival Mix, Chapter 10
   apple
   milk

Dinner
   Martians and More, Chapter 6
   Skywalk Trio, Chapter 4 *or* Sea Creature Pie, Chapter 4
   carrots *or* green beans
   Cosmic Cookies, Chapter 9
   milk

Astrofact: It takes the sun one cosmic year to make a trip around the galaxy. In five billion years the sun has only circled the galaxy about twenty times. So a cosmic year is a very long time.

Astrotip: When planning meals, remember to contrast colors and textures as you combine foods from the four groups. You wouldn't serve macaroni and cheese, sweet potatoes, whipped carrots, and oranges all in one meal— they're all soft foods and almost the same colors. That's almost as boring as eating Braxtl bread three times a day! A better combination would be macaroni and cheese with peas or broccoli or green beans, Mars Salad I, and an apple.

SUMMER MENUS

Breakfast
cantaloupe or fruit juice
Galactic Goop, Chapter 2
milk

Lunch
Star Melts, Chapter 7
Mars Salad II, *or* Mars Salad III, Chapter 6
Cave Rocks, Chapter 9

Dinner
Mars Salad I with Deimos Dressing, Chapter 6
carrots *or* corn on the cob
Venus Vittles, Chapter 4
Lunar Whip, Chapter 9

Astrofact: Mars' two small moons are called Phobos and Deimos. Phobos is closest to Mars and is about 15 miles in diameter. Deimos, the outer moon, is about 8 miles in diameter.

Astrotip: Mealtimes should be pleasant times. Set the table neatly, with fork and napkin to the left of the dinner plate, and knife, spoon, and drinking glass on the right. Serve hot foods hot and cold foods well chilled. Most of all—keep the conversation pleasant.

Astroriddle: The space traveler visited a cafe on Ganymede and found natives from many planets. There was a long-tailed Martian, two short-tailed Mercurians, and even a stubby-tailed Milky Way Swimmer. Which do you think ate and drank with his tail? *All of them. No animal removes its tail to eat and drink.*

AUTUMN MENUS

Breakfast
orange or fruit juice
Moon Plate *or* Weightless Pancakes, Chapter 2
milk

Lunch
Bug-eyed Monsters, Chapter 3
Blastoffs, Chapter 8 *or* Star Puffs, Chapter 3
Solar Debris, Chapter 10
milk

Dinner
Rings 'n Planets, Chapter 6
Satellite Supper I or II, Chapter 4
broccoli or green beans
Baked Planets, Chapter 9
milk

Astrofact: Venus flyby's have sent back information showing that planet to be veiled by thick clouds of carbon dioxide mixed with sulfuric acid. The planet has a high temperature and heavy air pressure. Football-field-size photographs taken straight down through the atmosphere revealed a surface covered with large boulders.

Astrotip: A seasonal centerpiece can brighten your dinner table—fresh flowers in spring, a bowl of fruit in summer, gourds and Indian corn in autumn, evergreens with pine cones or holly berries in winter.

187

Astroriddle: How can you keep from getting a sharp pain in the eye when you drink Zoom Soup on Venus? *Take the spoon out of the cup before drinking.*

WINTER MENUS

Breakfast
    banana or fruit juice
    Zoom Soup, Chapter 2
    Space Colony Biscuits, Chapter 7
    milk

Lunch
    raw carrot strips
    Space Dips, Chapter 8
    Inner Space Cookies, Chapter 9
    milk

Dinner
    Earth Green Salad, Chapter 6
    Star-Studded Ham, Chapter 4
    Booster Rockets, Chapter 5
    cauliflower *or* peas
    Solar Whip, Chapter 9
    milk

Astrofact: Some scientists believe it is possible that half the stars in our huge galaxy may have planets we have not yet been able to see. Since the Milky Way galaxy includes at least 100 billion stars—and there are millions of other galaxies, each with many millions of stars—there could be many undiscovered planets in the universe.

SPECIAL MEALS FOR SPECIAL DAYS

Breakfast
  fresh fruit in season
  Skywheel Omelet, Chapter 2
  Shuttle Muffins, Chapter 7
  milk

Lunch
  Lunar Cheese Salad, Chapter 6
  Star Puffs, Chapter 3
  Mars Muddle, Chapter 5
  Meteor Mounds, Chapter 10
  milk

Dinner
  Planetray, Chapter 3
  Moon Cheese Salad Balls, Chapter 6
  Space Lab Loaf, Chapter 4
  Starshine Ice Cream, Chapter 9
  milk
    or
  Black Holes, Chapter 3
  Mars Salad I, Chapter 6
  Sloppy Joe Volcanoes, Chapter 4
  spinach *or* green beans
  Mars Whip, Chapter 9
  milk

Astroriddle: Everyone in the astrocrew could see the Planetray except the astrocook. Why? *The cook was carrying the Planetray on his head.*

PICNIC MENUS

For summertime, try a picnic breakfast in the park.
Far-out Saucers with choice of fillings, Chapter 7
assorted fruits
Survival Mix, Chapter 10
milk

For anytime, enjoy a picnic lunch in the back yard.
Bug-eyed Monsters, Chapter 3
Night-Side Dip and dippers, Chapter 3
Leader Sandwiches, Chapter 8
Star Bubble Beverage, Chapter 11
Inner Space Cookies, *or* Cosmic Cookies, Chapter 9

For wintertime, set up a picnic supper before the fireplace.
Day-Side Dip and dippers, Chapter 3
Laser Mix, Chapter 6
Dark-Side Punch, Chapter 11
Creamy Planets, Chapter 9

Astrofact: On Earth we measure long distances in miles. But the universe is so tremendous, that if we tried to measure in miles the distance to stars other than the sun, we would have to use too many zeros—26,000,000,000,000 or 197,000,000,000,000,000. So astronomers measure distances by the speed of light instead of by miles. The speed of light is the distance light travels in one second—186,000 miles. (The star Alpha Centauri is 4.3 light years from Earth.)

MILKY WAY PUZZLE

Across:

5. _____ measure distances by the speed of light.
6. Some scientists believe that half the _____ in our huge galaxy may have planets we have not yet been able to see.
8. Name Mars' smaller moon.
9. Our solar system is in the Milky Way _____.

Down:

1. Name Mars' closer and larger moon.
2. An _____ should eat foods from the four basic food groups each day.
3. A galaxy is a system of _____.
4. The sun makes one trip _____ the galaxy in a cosmic year.
7. A wide variety of foods are needed to keep Earth's inhabitants in _____top condition.
10. Venus is veiled by thick clouds of carbon dioxide and sulfuric _____.

GALAXY GREATS
Gifts from the Kitchen

Star Wizard

Mona ran a comb through her bright-red hair and pulled on her Beta-cloth overalls. Through the window of the bungalow she saw bluebirds warbling in a willow tree.

"Lucky birds," she mumbled, "you never have to work."

"Hurry!" called Laurel. "You're late again!"

Mona grumbled as she trailed her sister to the elevator. "Work, work, work," she groaned as they rode through the tunnel to the ag-pods surrounding Star Colony One. "I thought we were gonna take it easy out here in space," she complained as they stepped out by the ag-pod where corn was growing.

"The first people to settle a new land always have to work hard," Laurel told her, "but it's worth it."

"Huh!" Mona snorted and waited for Laurel to roll back the airlock hatch on ag-pod three.

"Mmmm," Laurel sniffed as they stepped inside. "Don't these herbs smell good?"

"Yuk! I wish I could be a *bird*." Mona groaned. "Then I'd never have to smell them again."

Zing! She felt a tremble like the vibration of a bell. "What's shaking?" she asked. "The shuttle isn't due today is it?"

"I didn't feel anything." Laurel was busy snipping basil. "But Karalee says when the colony vibrates and it isn't the shuttle, that means the Star Wizard is here. Someone is going to get three wishes."

"Rubbish!" Mona snapped.

"Well I could use a wish or two," Laurel said. "I want to finish the basil in time to go to Karalee's party. And I really wish I had enough money to buy her a gift."

Mona made a face. "Karalee's bungalow smells like a barnyard. All those dirty pets in cages. Guinea pigs and—"

"I've cut four rows," Laurel interrupted. "Will you carry the herbs to the solar screens to dry?"

"I'm in no hurry." Mona slumped down on a bench and pulled out a comb and mirror. "Boy, if I really had three wishes, one of them would be to get rid of this awful *red hair*."

Zing! Mona jumped. "Hey! I felt it again!"

Laurel scooped up an armload of herbs. "Be careful. That's two wishes. If you make three while Star Wizard's here, they all come true."

"Rubbish!"

"Well if you don't believe it, I'll try my third wish. Because I really wish you'd stop—"

"Wait!" Mona shouted. "Me first, just in case! I wish I would *never, every have to work again!*"

Zing! Mona's skin tickled. Her scalp prickled. She felt as though she were shrinking. She put one hand on her head and felt—feathers? She looked down at her feet and saw—claws?

She looked for Laurel. But all she could see were shiny gold bars before her eyes. The last words she heard were her sister's.

"Mona! Where are you? I was only going to wish that you would stop complaining. But look—the basil is all cut and dried. And here on the bench is a small birdcage with a tag that says, FOR KARALEE.

"Mona? Look—there's a funny little bird inside with a bright red top knot. Mona? Where are you?"

Mona opened her mouth and groaned one last time before she began to chirp.

Astrofact: Our galaxy is the Milky Way galaxy. The Milky Way is only one of many billions of galaxies that make up our universe. A quasar is a galaxy that gives off tremendous energy from its central area, possibly from exploding stars. A pulsar is an object spinning rapidly in outer space, giving out regular short bursts of radio waves. It appears to be a neutron star spinning plasma clouds from a supernova. Fast spin "cracks the whip" so radio energy flies off the outer edge.

GALAXY GIFTS

There are galaxy-wide reasons for gift-giving and as many ideas for gifts. This chapter will suggest some ways to package, wrap, and give food gifts from Space Age recipes.

Astroriddle: What is forty feet long, has lots of hair, sings a lot, and always eats Space Spices? *A forty-foot, hairy, song-loving Space-Spice eater.*

☆ STAR WIZARD VINEGAR

Make tangy salad vinegar by adding herbs to cider vinegar and putting into clean empty bottles. Don't forget to add a label.

cider vinegar, red or white
dried herbs—choose from sweet basil, ruby-colored opal basil, tarragon, dill, or peppermint (good with fruit salad)

empty ketchup bottles
funnel
paper towels

Soak ketchup bottles in hot water until you can peel the labels off. Scrub well with hot soapy water, inside and out, and rinse thoroughly. Place upside down on dish rack to drain and dry.

Pick sprigs of herbs from the garden. They should be five or six inches long. (Fresh dill stalks are sometimes available in the market.) Wash herbs under cold running water, shake gently, and pat dry with paper towels. Push a sprig into each ketchup bottle.

Put the funnel in the bottle mouth. Ask a crew member to hold the funnel steady while you pour red or white cider vinegar over the sprig of herbs until the bottle is filled. Put the cap on and fasten it tightly.

Write the name of the herb vinegar on a card and tie it to the bottle neck with a ribbon. Or write the name on a gummed label from a stationery store and stick it to the bottle front. Place the vinegars in the back of a dark cupboard for at least one month. Flavors will blend better if you can keep the vinegars in the dark for three months. (If you plan them for Christmas giving, you should make them in September.)

☆ SPACE SPICES

Blend combinations of spices for special flavoring. Package them in pretty containers and add tips for their use.

SPACE SPICE I

2 tbsp dry mustard
2 tbsp dry lemon peel
4 tsp ground allspice
4 tsp ground nutmeg
4 tsp ground ginger
2 tsp salt
2 tsp pepper
2 tsp cayenne

large jar with lid
small containers with lids

Small containers may be empty mustard jars or baby food jars or other small jar with a tight-fitting lid. Soak to peel off any labels. Wash well, then dry thoroughly.

Combine all spices in a large covered jar. Shake well to

196

blend thoroughly. Put into small containers. Store in dark cupboard. Add astrotip to recipe card: Space Spice Mix I is great blended in tomato soup, chili, pork stew, or added to hamburgers.

☆ SPACE SPICE II

3 tbsp celery salt
3 tbsp garlic salt
3 tbsp onion salt
1½ tsp paprika
1½ tsp chili powder
½ tsp pepper
¼ tsp cayenne

large jar with lid
small jars with lids

Wash small glass jars, soaking labels as directed above. Drain and dry. Combine all spices in large covered jar, put lid on tightly, and shake well to blend all spices. Pour into small dry containers and store in dark cupboard. Add astrotip to recipe card: Space Spice Mix II is good sprinkled over meat, fish, or vegetables.

Astroriddle: What happened when the lady space captain found a goat hidden in the astrocook's new icebox? *The goat turned to butt 'er.*

GALAXY BUTTERS

Mix softened butter or margarine with flavorings shortly before gift-giving time. Store in covered containers in refrigerator. They'll keep for three weeks.

☆ GALAXY BUTTER I

½ cup softened butter or
  margarine
2 tbsp honey
1 tsp grated orange peel
½ tsp ground ginger

bowl
grater
measuring spoons
measuring cup
mixing spoon
small containers with lids

Wash and dry empty containers (margarine tubs, small cottage cheese cartons, sour cream cartons, or similar containers).

To grate orange peel, wash and dry a fresh orange. Be sure to keep your fingers away from the sharp grater edges. Cup your hand around the orange and rub it away from you on the grater. Keep turning the orange so you grate the colored peel, but not the white pulp beneath.

Put the softened butter or margarine into a bowl, add the orange peel and spices, and stir well to blend. Spoon into prepared containers and cover with lid. Write recipe on a gummed label and stick to front of container. Refrigerate. Add astrotip to recipe label: Use Galaxy Butter I on cooked carrots, sweet potatoes, or spread on Battlestar Bread slices or other breads made with raisins, bananas, or dates.

☆☆ GALAXY BUTTER II

2 tbsp sesame seeds
½ cup softened butter or
  margarine
½ tsp garlic salt

small skillet
potholders or mitts
mixing spoon
measuring cup
measuring spoons
bowl
small containers with lids

Put sesame seeds into skillet. Place over medium-low heat. Hold skillet handle with hot pad or mitt and stir seeds as they cook until they become golden brown. Turn off heat. Use potholder or mitt and pour seeds into bowl to cool.

Add butter or margarine and garlic salt to cooled seeds and stir well to blend. Spoon into gift containers, then refrigerate. Add astrotip to recipe label: This butter mixture is good on green vegetables or toasted French bread.

Astrofact: The entire universe of galaxies is called a metagalaxy. It includes billions of galaxies, each containing billions of stars!

☆ GALAXY BUTTER III

½ cup softened butter or
  margarine
1 tsp chili powder
½ tsp garlic salt

bowl
mixing spoon
measuring cup
measuring spoons
containers with lids

Put softened butter or margarine into bowl, add spices, and stir well to blend flavors. Spoon into covered containers and refrigerate. When gift-giving, add recipe with astrotip: Galaxy Butter III is good spread over corn on the cob, hot French bread, or baked potatoes.

Astrofact: Our closest star, the sun, is so near the Earth we can measure the distance by miles (93 million). But the next closest star, Alpha Centauri, is 26,000,000,000,000 miles away (26 trillion miles). It is easier to measure that distance as astronomers do and say that Alpha Centauri is 4⅓ light years from Earth. (It takes 4⅓ years for light from that star to travel to Earth.) All the other stars you see twinkling in space at night are even farther away than that. The light you see coming from the constellation called Cassiopeia left there when Earth was in the Ice Age. During all those centuries, that light has been traveling toward Earth and only now has come close enough for us to see it.

Astroriddles: L5 is an area favored for space colonies to be located between Earth and the moon. Can you answer these riddles using other letter and number combinations?

What letter and number say what the crew has finished after leaving the astrocook's dining hall? *E10 (eaten).*
What two letters describe any dessert on Pluto? *IC (icy).*
What two letters describe a space colonist's garden just after planting? *CD (seedy).*
What letters describe the largest areas of the planet Earth? *C's (seas).*
What two letters describe an astrocook's galley before supplies come aboard? *MT (empty).*
What letter and number tell what the astrocook did to the eggs before adding them to Shuttle Muffins? *B10 (beaten).*

SPACE AGE GIFT IDEAS
FROM OTHER CHAPTERS

Any of these would welcome a new neighbor, cheer a sick friend, or please anybody special at any time!

Astrofact: Icarus in Greek mythology flew on wings attached with wax which melted when he flew too near the sun. Icarus in space is an asteroid with an orbit that brings it closer to the sun than the planet Mercury.

SPACE-STYLE CONTAINERS

Your gift foods should be put together to look their most delicious when you give them to friends. Here are some ideas to get you started.

EMPTY BOTTLES

Make an exploration of your own kitchen. Are there almost empty bottles in the cupboard and refrigerator? Put a rubber band around the neck to remind your crew to save the bottles when they're empty.

Soak empty bottles in hot water until you can peel the labels away. Wash bottles with hot soapy water, rinse inside and outside, and place upside down on draining rack to dry. Bottles and jars must be absolutely dry inside before you add dry mixtures such as Space Spices, Solar Debris, or Survival Mixes.

Ketchup bottles are good for Star Wizard Vinegar. So are salad dressing bottles, small vinegar bottles, or any other small bottle with a narrow neck.

Space Spices should be put into small containers such as baby food jars, instant coffee jars, small mustard jars, or empty spice jars.

Empty peanut butter jars can hold Survival Mixes, Solar Debris, Galaxy Butters, Cave Rocks, Cosmic Cookies, Inner Space Cookies, or Solar Fruit Strips rolled in plastic wrap. Soak the label from the jar, wash in hot soapy water, and dry thoroughly. See *Space Wraps* for ways to decorate.

Plastic containers are great for Galaxy Butters, Survival Mixes, Solar Debris, Inner Space or Cosmic Cookies, or Cave Rocks. Ask your crew to save all margarine tubs, cottage cheese, yogurt, sour cream, and similar cartons. Wash in hot soapy water and dry thoroughly.

You'll find other containers in your kitchen. What will you give in coffee cans, oatmeal cartons, or potato chip tubes?

FLYING SAUCER GIFTS

Start with a heavy paper or plastic plate. Have plastic wrap and ribbons on hand. Here are some suggested combinations of Space Age gift foods—you'll probably think of more.

SURVIVAL MIX COMBO

Pile paper plate with a mound of Survival Mix I, II, or III. Spread Solar Debris around the edge. Place plate on plastic wrap, pull edges over plate, and hold together in the middle. Tie tightly with a wire twistee, then tie on bright ribbons and bows. Remember to write the recipe on a card, poke a hole in one corner, and tie it to the ribbon.

Cooky and Candy Combo: Arrange Cave Rock candies with Cosmic Cookies and Inner Space Cookies. Place plastic wrap over the top, pull beneath the plate, and press edges together. Put a bright bow in the center of the plate.

Crackers and Cheese Combo: Pile Landing Pad Crackers or Cheese Meteors in the center, scatter Sun Flakes around the edges, cover with plastic wrap and add a bright bow.

Or mix and match the suggestions above. Arrange Solar Debris or Survival Mix around the edge of a plate piled with Cheese Meteors.

Astrofact: A comet is made of meteoroidal materials frosted with frozen gas. Comets move in long orbits around the sun. Comet tails are made of gas so thin stars can be seen through them. Someone once described a comet tail as something as close to nothing as anything can be and still be something. They're blown by the solar wind and can be 100 million miles long.

SPACE WRAPS

A comet's tail is so thin you can see stars through it. Why not make comet tail wrap for your gifts? Paste colored stick-on stars on the bottle, jar, paper plate, or other container. Wrap with a strip of plastic film, tie with a wire twistee, then tie again with a brightly colored ribbon.

Astrofact: In 1910, the Earth moved through the tail of Halley's comet with no bad effects, though some people thought it would bring the end of the world. Halley's comet will come our way again early in 1986. Scientists at NASA plan to send up a spacecraft for a close view.

BOTTLED GIFTS

For Star Wizard Vinegar, just tie a bow around the bottle neck. Put your friend's name on one side of a card and write the recipe on the other side. Decorate the card with stars and crescent moons or paste on stick-on stars. Poke a hole through one corner of the card, thread it onto one end of the ribbon around the bottle neck, and tie securely.

JARS WITH LIDS

Paint the lids with bright colors and let dry before using. Or trace the jar lid on the wrong side of colorful paper—you might use gift wrap, foil, construction paper, a page of the Sunday comics, or a bright illustration torn from a magazine (ask permission, of course). Cut out the circle and glue to the top of the jar lid. Tie a ribbon around the neck of the jar. Write the recipe for the star gift, poke a hole through the recipe card, thread it through the ribbon, and tie.

Or cut star shapes from illustrations in old magazines. Glue all over the lid. Tie with ribbon and recipe as suggested above.

TUBS, CARTONS AND OTHER WAXED CONTAINERS

Decorate lids with circles cut from colored contact papers.

Or fill cartons, place on piece of gift wrap, Sunday comic, or other bright paper, pull edges to the top, hold together, tie with a wire twistee, then tie again with bright ribbon.

Astrofact: Our sun is young, though it is about 5 billion years old. Scientists believe the universe, as a whole, is at least 10 billion years old.

Astroquestion: Scientists are learning exciting things about our great solar system. Some of these things are sill "learned guesses." That means that scientists decide a thing is true by studying all the information available. But sometimes new information shows that the learned guesses were wrong.

When the Apollo Lander sent back information from the moon, scientists discovered that some learned guesses were almost as incorrect as the old saying that the moon was made of green cheese.

Many mysteries remain in our universe. Many learned guesses are still to be proved true or untrue. Perhaps one day *you* will help solve some of those mysteries.

GALAXY PUZZLE

Across:

3. Pulsars are radio waves, probably spun from what kind of star?
4. Name of our next closest star. (two words)
8. A comet's tail is very _____.
9. Traveling space debris coated with frozen gas, or "dirty snowball."
11. Icarus in Greek mythology flew on wings attached with what material?
12. Jupiter and Saturn are two _____ planets.
13. What the moon is not made of.

Down:

1. The entire universe of galaxies is called a _____.
2. You can see these through a comet's tail.
5. The Milky Way galaxy is shaped like what child's toy?
6. An exploding star is called a _____.
7. The light we see left Alpha Centauri when Earth was still in what time period? (two words)
10. A planet's loop around the sun is called an _____.
14. Another word for a star.

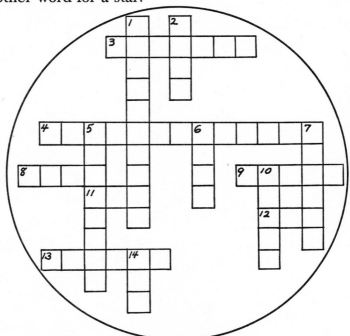

PUZZLE SOLUTIONS

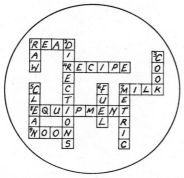

Starship Starters Puzzle Solution

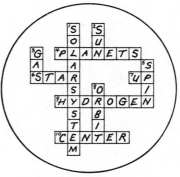

Sun Puzzle Solution

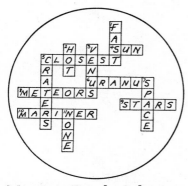

Mercury Puzzle Solution

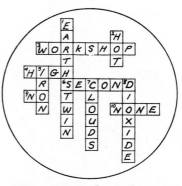

Venus Puzzle Solution

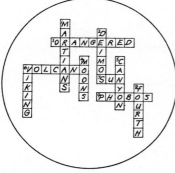

Earth Puzzle Solution

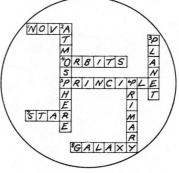

Mars Puzzle Solution

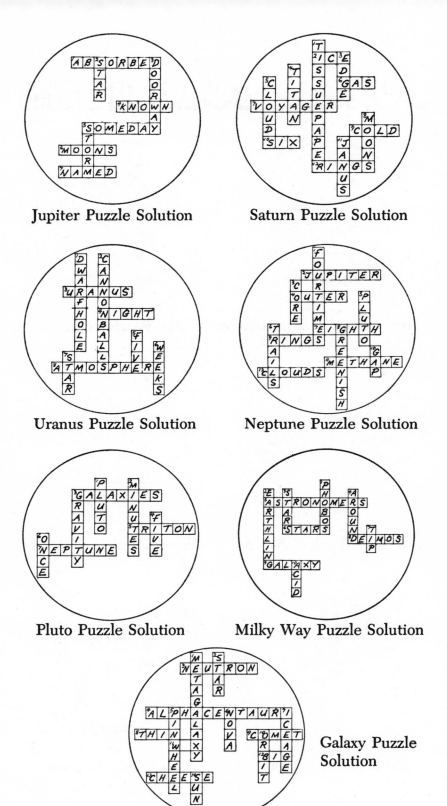

Jupiter Puzzle Solution

Saturn Puzzle Solution

Uranus Puzzle Solution

Neptune Puzzle Solution

Pluto Puzzle Solution

Milky Way Puzzle Solution

Galaxy Puzzle Solution

BIBLIOGRAPHY

SCIENCE FACT

Adams, Florence. *Catch a Sunbeam*. New York: Harcourt Brace Jovanovich, 1978.

Asimov, Isaac. *How Did We Find Out About Outer Space?* New York: Walker and Co., 1977.

———. *How Did We Find Out About Vitamins?* New York: Walker and Co., 1974.

———. *Words of Science and the History Behind Them*. Boston: Houghton Mifflin Co., 1959.

Bergaust, Erik, ed. *The New Illustrated Space Encyclopedia*. New York: G. P. Putnam's Sons, 1970.

Bova, Ben. *Starflight and Other Improbabilities*. Philadelphia: The Westminster Press, 1973.

Branley, Franklyn M. *A Book of Planets for You*. New York: Thomas Y. Crowell Co., 1966.

———. *Pieces of Another World: The Story of Moon Rocks*. New York: Thomas Y. Crowell Co., 1972.

Cobb, Jerrie, with Jane Rieker. *Woman into Space: The Jerrie Cobb Story*. Englewood Cliffs: Prentice-Hall, Inc., 1963.

Cronie, William J. *Skylab*. New York: David McKay Co. Inc., 1976.

Feravolo, Rocco V. *Easy Physics Projects: Air, Water & Heat*. Englewood Cliffs: Prentice-Hall, Inc., 1966.

Gallant, Roy A. *Beyond Earth: The Search for Extraterrestrial Life.* New York: Four Winds Press, 1977.

————. *Fires in the Sky: The Birth and Death of Stars.* New York: Four Winds Press, 1977.

Golden, Frederick. *Colonies in Space: The Next Giant Step.* New York: Harcourt Brace Jovanovich, 1977.

Jacobs, Lou, Jr. *Space Station '80.* New York: Hawthorn Books, Inc., 1973.

Knight, David C. *Eavesdropping on Space: The Quest of Radio Astronomy.* New York: William Morrow and Co., 1974.

————. *32 Moons: Natural Satellites of our Solar System.* New York: William Morrow and Co., 1974.

————. *The Tiny Planets: Asteroids of our Solar System.* New York: William Morrow and Co., 1973.

Milgrom, Harry. *First Experiments with Gravity.* New York: E. P. Dutton & Co., Inc., 1966.

Moore, Patrick. *Seeing Stars.* New York: Rand McNally, 1971.

St. John, George. *How to Count Like a Martian.* New York: Henry Z. Walck Inc., 1975.

Stone, A. Harris and Bertram M. Siegel. *Take a Balloon.* Englewood Cliffs: Prentice-Hall, Inc., 1967.

Wheat, Janis Knudsen. *Let's Go to the Moon.* National Geographic Society, 1977.

Zim, Herbert S. *The Universe.* New York: William Morrow and Co., 1973.

SCIENCE FICTION ANTHOLOGIES

Brodkin, Sylvia Z. and Elizabeth J. Pearson, eds. *Science Fiction.* New York: Lothrop, Lee & Shepard Company, 1973.

A collection of science fiction stories, poems, and paintings which explore dimensions of time and space, alien life forms, and other themes, with well-known authors such as Isaac Asimov, Kurt Vonnegut, Jr., Arthur C. Clarke, and many more.

Carr, Terry, ed. *The Infinite Arena.* Nashville: Thomas Nelson Inc., 1977.

Seven science fiction stories about sports.

Elwood, Roger, ed. *Children of Infinity.* New York: Franklin Watts, 1973.

Eleven stories of children who inhabit future worlds. All original stories by well-known science fiction writers.

Ginnsburg, Mirra, ed. *The Air of Mars and Other Stories of Time and Space.* New York: Macmillan Publishing Company Inc., 1976.

A collection of fantasy and science fiction from the Soviet Union, ranging from serious to fantastic and from humorous to satiric.

Silverberg, Robert, ed. *Earth Is the Strangest Planet.* Nashville: Thomas Nelson Inc. 1977.

Ten stories of science fiction.

Yolen, Jane, ed. *Shape Shifters.* New York: Seabury Press, 1978.

Fantasy and science fiction stories—from eerie to humorous— about humans who can change their shapes.

————. *Zoo 2000, Twelve Stories of Science Fiction and Fantasy Beasts.* New York: Seabury Press, 1973.

Twelve stories to suggest the relationship between humans and animals in the future by such well-known science fiction authors as Theodore Sturgeon, Larry Niven, and Philip José Farmer.

SCIENCE FICTION POETRY AND MISCELLANY

Brewton, Sara and John E. and John Brewton Blackburn, eds. *Of Quarks, Quasars and Other Quirks: Quizzical Poems for the Supersonic Age.* New York: Thomas Y. Crowell Co., 1977.

SCIENCE FICTION FOR YOUNGER READERS

Asimov, Isaac. *The Heavenly Host.* New York: Walker and Co., 1975.

Story set in the Christmas season wherein a boy from Earth teaches adults to respect alien creatures.

Morressy, John. *The Humans of Ziax II.* New York: Walker and Co., 1974.

A boy from Earth learns nonviolence from aliens while exploring another planet.

Norton, Andre and Michael Gilbert. *The Day of the Ness.* New York: Walker and Co., 1975.

A boy from Earth helps alien creatures.

Robison, Nancy. *UFO KIDNAP!* New York: Lothrop, Lee & Shepard Company, 1978.

Two boys are trapped inside when UFO takes off, but outsmart their captors and navigate the UFO back to Earth in a funny and exciting story.

SCIENCE FICTION FOR INTERMEDIATE READERS

Beatty, Jerome, Jr. *Matthew Looney in the Outback.* New York: W. R. Scott, 1969.

————. *Matthew Looney's Invasion of the Earth.* New York: W. R. Scott, 1965.

————. *Matthew Looney's Voyage to the Earth.* New York: W. R. Scott, 1961.

Humorous, "punny" adventures of a moon boy who believes there is life on Earth.

Lightner, A. M. *Star Dog*. New York: McGraw-Hill Book Company, 1973.

> Born of Earth mother and alien father, telepathic dog involves his young owner in humorously told mystery.

———. *The Thursday Toads*. New York: McGraw-Hill Book Company, 1971.

> When Gillian Abbott, a young Ph.D., is bitten by a dread Toxic Toad and survives, he's sent to Thursday planet to help eradicate the deadly creatures . . . and succeeds all too well.

Norton, Andre. *Outside*. New York: Walker and Co., 1974.

> Girl on Earth seeks escape from dying domed city to Outside, said to be poisoned by pollution.

———. *Star Ka'at*. New York: Walker and Co., 1976.

> Earth children are saved from planet's self-destruction by cats from outer space.

Slote, Alfred. *My Trip to Alpha I*. Philadelphia: J. B. Lippincott Company, 1978.

> A boy travels from Earth to Alpha I by a transportation system that uses dummies of people reconstructed by computer card data— and discovers a sinister scheme against his wealthy mine-owner aunt.

SCIENCE FICTION FOR OLDER READERS

Christopher, John. *The City of Gold and Lead*. New York: Macmillan Publishing Company, 1967.

———. *The Pool of Fire*. New York: Macmillan Publishing Company, 1968.

———. *The White Mountains*. New York: Macmillan Publishing Company, 1967.

> Trilogy set a century ahead when Earth is ruled by Tripods and three boys set out to free it.

———. *The Lotus Caves*. New York: Macmillan Publishing Company, 1969.

> Teenagers find more than they bargained for while exploring outside their lunar dome.

Gregorian, Joyce Ballou. *Castledown*. New York: Atheneum, 1977.

> A girl struggles to free Tredana from usurpers.

Hoover, H. M. *Children of Morrow*. New York: Four Winds Press, 1973.

> Two children, with psychic abilities unlike others in their village, follow dream directions to escape pursuers and join their own people.

————. *The Delikon*. New York: The Viking Press, Inc., 1977.

Varina is caught between warring humans and the Delikon.

Key, Alexander. *Escape to Witch Mountain*. Philadelphia: The Westminster Press, 1968.

"Different" children escape orphanage and pursuit to find their own kind.

L'Engle, Madeleine. *A Wrinkle in Time*. New York: Farrar, Straus and Giroux, Inc., 1962.

Two children rescue their father from a force imprisoning him.

————. *A Wind in the Door*. New York: Farrar, Straus and Giroux, Inc., 1973. (Sequel)

————. *A Swiftly Tilting Planet*. New York: Farrar, Strauss and Giroux, Inc., 1978. (Sequel)

McCaffrey, Ann. *Dragonsong*. New York: Atheneum, 1976.

A future world where dragons are raised as defense against deadly "threads."

————. *Dragonsinger*. New York. Atheneum, 1977. (Sequel)

Silverberg, Robert. *Worlds' Fair, 1992*. Chicago, Follett Publishing Co., 1970.

Teenager wins trip to work for one year at World's Fair satellite and gets in on exploratory trip to Pluto.

Sleator, William. *House of Stairs*. New York: E. P. Dutton and Co. Inc., 1974.

Five orphans try to understand and survive mysterious imprisonment on unending series of stairs and platforms.

Townsend, John Rowe. *Noah's Castle*. Philadelphia: J. B. Lippincott Co., 1975.

Story of the various ways British citizens react to severe food shortages in the not-too-distant future.

INDEX